D1415940

FUEL UNDER FIRE

PETROLEUM AND ITS PERILS

MARGARET J. GOLDSTEIN

TFCB TWENTY-FIRST CENTURY BOOKS
MINNEAPOLIS

TO JACKIE, WHO PUTS UP WITH ALL MY STUPID IDEAS
—M.J.G.

Twenty-First Century Books
A division of Lerner Publishing Group, Inc.
241 First Avenue North
Minneapolis, MN 55401 USA

Main body text set in Caecilia Com 10/15.
Typeface provided by Linotype AG.

For reading levels and more information, look up this title at www.lernerbooks.com.

Library of Congress Cataloging-in-Publication Data

Goldstein, Margaret J.
    Fuel under fire : petroleum and its perils / by Margaret J. Goldstein.
        pages   cm
    Includes bibliographical references and index.
    Audience: Age 12–18.
    ISBN 978-1-4677-3831-6 (lib. bdg. : alk. paper)
    ISBN 978-1-4677-8802-1 (EB pdf)
    1. Petroleum—Juvenile literature. I. Title.
    TN870.3.G65 2016
    338.2'728—dc23   2014020890

Manufactured in the United States of America
1 – PC – 7/15/15

CONTENTS

CHAPTER ONE

BLACK GOLD

"It was a big pop, a loud bang sound, and I didn't think anything about it," Jennifer Whittington told a reporter in Mayflower, Arkansas, in 2013. "About five minutes later I came out and there was the river of oil."

A river of oil? In the little town of Mayflower? How could this be? Where did the oil come from?

Unbeknownst to most residents of Mayflower, oil had flowed through their town for many years. It traveled underground, through the Pegasus pipeline, operated by the Texas-based ExxonMobil Corporation. For more than sixty years, the Pegasus had carried oil from wells in Texas through Arkansas and north to refineries in Illinois. By the early 2000s, oil companies had also tapped vast supplies of oil in Alberta, Canada. To get that oil south to the United States, ExxonMobil and other companies sent it through the Pegasus and other established pipelines.

The oil that comes from Alberta is heavier and thicker than oil from other regions. It has the consistency of peanut butter. To make it more liquid, so it will flow through pipes, oil companies mix it with benzene, hydrogen sulfide, and other chemicals. That's the kind of oil that was flowing beneath Mayflower on March 29, 2013, when the Pegasus pipeline broke. Oil came spurting up through a 22-foot-long (6.7-meter) gash in the pipe. It flowed into people's backyards. It pooled in neighborhood streets. Some oil flowed down a storm sewer and into a lake near town. In wooded areas, ducks and turtles got stuck in the thick black goo. The animals tried to clean the oil from their skin and feathers by grooming themselves, but in the process they ingested oil.

Along with the oil came a strong, bitter smell. Residents panicked and called the police. The authorities evacuated townspeople from

Emergency crews in Mayflower, Arkansas, tackle the cleanup of a Canadian crude oil spill in March 2013. The oil—and the hazardous chemicals it contained to keep it in liquid form—polluted the land and sickened animals and people in the affected area.

twenty-two homes in the neighborhood at the center of the spill. Workers arrived in hazmat (hazardous materials) suits. In the following days and weeks, workers stopped the leak and cleared away the pools of oil.

All around town, though, the air still reeked of tar. In many spots, an oily film remained on the ground and in the water. Many animals were sickened by the oil they'd ingested, and more than two hundred of them died. Town residents began to complain of headaches, stomachaches, rashes, and breathing problems. They worried that the benzene and other toxic chemicals in the oil had made them sick. Many people tried to sell their homes so they could move out of town—but no one wanted to buy them.

ExxonMobil provided some assistance. It paid to clean up the spill, covered the medical bills of some sick residents, and offered to buy sixty-two houses in the area of the oil spill so that residents could move elsewhere. It also paid a US government fine of $2.6 million for failing to properly maintain the Pegasus pipeline. Still, many locals and industry critics said that ExxonMobil hadn't done enough to help Mayflower residents. They also said the company should have taken more precautions to ensure the structural integrity of its pipeline so that oil would not leak on its journey from Canada. Critics further pointed out that the fine ExxonMobil paid to the government was tiny compared to the company's $44 billion yearly profits.

It's no surprise that people were upset after the Mayflower spill. After all, no one wants oil pooling in public streets or contaminating the water. No one wants to breathe in toxic fumes from oil. No one wants to see animals and birds killed by oil.

But everyone wants oil.

OIL, OIL EVERYWHERE

The world runs on oil. Every day, people on Earth use 90 million barrels (about 3.7 billion gallons, or 14 billion liters) of oil. Cars, airplanes, farm equipment, and buses run on oil. Many people heat their homes with oil. Oil is used in the manufacture of millions of products, from detergent to paint to plastics.

Another name for oil is petroleum. Though these two terms are often used interchangeably, petroleum ("rock oil" in Latin) actually exists in three forms: liquid, solid, and gas. The liquid form is crude oil, the solid form is bitumen, and the gaseous form is natural gas. All three forms are used around the world in thousands of ways. The petroleum business—which includes the extraction, processing, transport, and sale of petroleum in all its forms—is a multibillion-dollar industry that employs millions of people worldwide. Different forms of petroleum are burned to heat homes, run cars, and power machinery.

How much petroleum have you used today? Perhaps you're thinking: "I drove to school today, and the car runs on gasoline, so I used a little petroleum today."

The correct answer, however, is that you used a lot of petroleum today. Yes, a car runs on gasoline, a petroleum product, but the four tires on that car are also made partly of petroleum. The roads between home and school are probably made of asphalt, a form of bitumen. The clothes you're wearing—if they contain any synthetic fibers, such as nylon or acrylic—are made partly of petroleum. The detergent used to wash them was probably made with petroleum as well. And the rest of your daily routine likely also depends on petroleum.

Especially in the United States—where petroleum and its by-products are plentiful and affordable—petroleum makes life comfortable. Americans can speed down the highway at 60 miles (120 kilometers) per hour in a gasoline-powered car. In a jet-fuel-powered airplane, passengers can fly from New York to California in a few hours. With a furnace run on natural gas or heating oil, people can be warm at home and relax with hot showers. Farmers use petroleum-based fertilizers and pesticides on their fields and harvest their crops with machines that run on diesel fuel, which is made from crude oil. Petroleum-powered trains, trucks, and ships bring foods from all over the world to US supermarkets. And petrochemicals—chemicals derived from petroleum—form the basis of products made partially or completely of plastic, including telephones, computers, backpacks, sunglasses, jewelry, toothbrushes, food containers, headphones, refrigerator magnets, ballpoint pens, and shampoo bottles, to name only a few.

Petroleum is at the heart of everyday conveniences, as economist Donald J. Boudreaux has pointed out:

> How many of us reflect on the benefits that we enjoy from asphalt? Asphalt makes road construction and repair less costly. So we in the industrialized world daily drive to school, work and play on clean, smooth roads that would not exist, or that would be less smooth and wide, were it not for this unassuming product made from petroleum. . . . The same is true for, say, plastic wrap. We give this stuff nary a thought. Yet because bacteria cannot pass through it, those thin sheets of plastic keep meats, vegetables, dairy products and breads fresher—and protect us against food poisoning.

If you look at a plastic bag, a bottle of detergent, a flame in a gas heater, or a can of motor oil, it's difficult to imagine that all these products come from the same resource—and that this resource existed long before it became part of the fabric of modern society.

In the 1930s, the Utah-based Sinclair Oil Corporation wanted a captivating logo to display in advertisements, at service stations around the United States, and on other company materials. A clever advertising team came up with a dinosaur. The idea was that the oil sold by Sinclair was older than the dinosaurs. In fact, that's true. The oil that we use to power vehicles, heat homes, and make petroleum-based products formed deep underground hundreds of millions of years ago.

The process began with ancient plankton, algae, and other tiny marine animals and plants. These creatures floated on the surface of ancient oceans and other waterways. When they died, their bodies settled in layers on the seafloor. Bacteria ate away some of the chemical substances in their remains, leaving mostly carbon and hydrogen behind. Over time, the remains were covered by sand and mud. As thousands and then millions of years went by, more sand and mud and dead creatures piled up. The remains of the tiny sea creatures were eventually buried several miles deep.

The lowest layers of sand and mud were under great pressure from the layers above. Over millions of years, that pressure and the heat it generated turned the lowest layers of sand and mud into rock. Meanwhile, the intense heat created chemical changes in the carbon-rich remains of the ancient sea creatures, turning them into a fossil fuel called petroleum.

THE BUILDING BLOCKS OF FOSSIL FUELS

All fossil fuels are made of hydrocarbons, different combinations of the chemical elements carbon and hydrogen. Hydrocarbons take various forms depending on the amounts of carbon and hydrogen in the mixture. For instance, a molecule of methane—gaseous hydrocarbon and the main ingredient in natural gas—consists of a single carbon atom and four hydrogen atoms. Hydrocarbons with five or more carbon atoms per molecule exist as liquids, such as crude oil. If the molecules are very large, the hydrocarbons take solid forms, such as coal.

PETROLEUM FORMATION

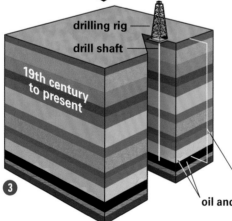

Tiny sea plants and animals died and came to rest on the ocean floor. Over time, they were covered by layers of silt and sand.

ocean 300–400 million years ago

1
sand and silt
plants and animals
plant and animal remains

Over millions of years, the remains were buried deeper and deeper. The pressure from the upper layers produced heat that turned the remains into oil and gas.

ocean 50–100 million years ago

2
sand and silt
plant and animal remains

drilling rig
drill shaft

19th century to present

In modern times, energy companies drill down through layers of sand, silt, and rock to reach the rock formations that contain oil and gas deposits.

3
sand, silt, and rock
oil and gas deposits

Earth has undergone tremendous changes over millions of years, and some places that were once covered by water have become dry land. Thus petroleum—the remains of sea creatures—might be found in inland areas that were once seas, as well as under existing seas. To get that petroleum, oil and gas companies search all over the planet—from northernmost Canada to deep under the ocean. Once they've located petroleum, companies drill deep into the ground or under the ocean floor to reach it. They then pump it to the surface and ship it to refineries, where it is processed to create fuels and other petroleum-based products.

At refineries, workers treat petroleum in its various forms—crude oil, bitumen, and natural gas—using intense heat, high pressure, and powerful chemicals. These processes remove impurities from the petroleum and separate it into its different fractions, or chemical components. The fractions are treated further to create different fuels, such as gasoline, kerosene, heating oil, and diesel fuel. Some fractions are

This oil refinery in Torrance, California, processes an average of 155,000 barrels (6.8 billion liters) of crude oil per day and produces 1.8 billion gallons of gasoline per year.

used to make petrochemicals, which are the basis for detergents, fertilizers, paint, plastics, synthetic fibers, and synthetic rubber. During refining, natural gas is often compressed and cooled, a procedure that turns it into liquid. This liquefied natural gas (LNG) takes up about six hundred times less space than ordinary natural gas. That makes it easier to store and transport. From refineries, LNG is shipped long distances, turned back into gas, and used as a heat and power source.

The United States consumes more than 20 percent of the oil used on Earth each day.

PETROLEUM FOR THE PEOPLE

Dependence on petroleum is greatest in industrialized nations such as the United States. In fact, the United States consumes more than 20 percent of the oil used on Earth each day. As US president George W. Bush said in his 2006 State of the Union address, "America is addicted to oil."

Petroleum, therefore, plays a major role in the US economy. According to the American Petroleum Institute (API), an alliance of oil and gas businesses, more than 2.5 million Americans are directly employed in the oil and gas industry—with jobs at oil wells, in oil refineries, and in oil pipeline construction. And that figure doesn't include other jobholders whose work is somehow connected to petroleum: car salespeople; auto mechanics; truck drivers; airline pilots; farmers; people who build and repair roads; and sellers of paints, pesticides, and plastic packaging. One way or another, most of the US economy is linked to petroleum.

Oil and gas companies also pump money into the international economy. These companies pay taxes to national, state, and local governments; hire subcontractors to build lengthy pipelines and massive refineries; pay rental money and fees to owners of the land where gas and oil wells are drilled; and pay geologists to search all over the world for new supplies of petroleum. Oil and gas companies also reap enormous profits worldwide. Of the ten most profitable companies in the world in 2013, four were oil companies. ExxonMobil led the top ten with $44 billion in yearly profits.

With so much oil money changing hands, petroleum has become known as black gold. And with all the petroleum flowing from beneath Earth's surface and eventually into our vehicles, buildings, and factories, it's no wonder that scholars call the past century and a half the Age of Oil.

THE DARK SIDE

Alongside its many benefits, petroleum presents its share of drawbacks. It is not a renewable resource—that is, it can't be replenished by short-term ecological cycles. It will take millions of years for Earth to create more petroleum through natural processes. Meanwhile, many of Earth's most easily accessed petroleum deposits have been used up. Companies have begun to search for oil in more difficult-to-reach places, such as deep under the oceans and near the North Pole, where melting ice caps are revealing previously inaccessible sources of oil. Experts disagree about when Earth's oil will be completely depleted, especially since new reserves are constantly being uncovered. But the search for more petroleum deposits and the methods of extracting those deposits are often environmentally destructive.

Petroleum-related accidents pose problems as well. Oil spills, such as the 2010 *Deepwater Horizon* accident in the Gulf of Mexico, during which more than 200 million gallons (757 million liters) of crude oil from a leaking well flowed into the Gulf over the course of eighty-seven days, can contaminate soil and water, kill wildlife, and make people sick. Drilling for and processing oil can also contaminate soil and groundwater. And plastics made from oil are a major source of pollution. Billions of tons of discarded plastic, which does not decompose, sit in landfills. When improperly discarded, plastics often end up in lakes and the oceans, where they harm wildlife.

On an even larger scale, the burning of fossil fuels—which provide 85 percent of Earth's energy—releases large amounts of carbon dioxide into the air. Carbon dioxide is known as a greenhouse gas because it traps the sun's heat in the atmosphere, much like the glass roof of a greenhouse traps the sun's rays. Increased levels of carbon dioxide in the air have caused Earth's average temperature to rise, triggering a major shift in the planet's climate.

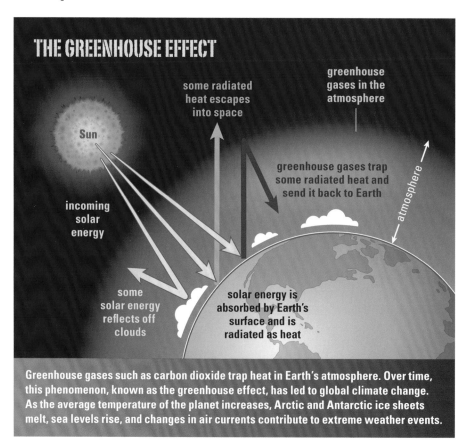

THE GREENHOUSE EFFECT

greenhouse gases in the atmosphere

some radiated heat escapes into space

Sun

greenhouse gases trap some radiated heat and send it back to Earth

atmosphere

incoming solar energy

some solar energy reflects off clouds

solar energy is absorbed by Earth's surface and is radiated as heat

Greenhouse gases such as carbon dioxide trap heat in Earth's atmosphere. Over time, this phenomenon, known as the greenhouse effect, has led to global climate change. As the average temperature of the planet increases, Arctic and Antarctic ice sheets melt, sea levels rise, and changes in air currents contribute to extreme weather events.

HOT TODAY

Scientists say that climate change is well under way. Consider just one week in mid-March 2012, when a heat wave hit the Upper Midwest. Temperatures in southeastern Michigan measured 30°F (17°C) above normal, and Chicago, Illinois, had the hottest Saint Patrick's Day ever recorded in 141 years of record keeping. Temperatures soared to 81°F (27°C)—41°F (23°C) above normal—in Bismarck, North Dakota. Winner, South Dakota, hit an astounding 94°F (34°C). And the trend has continued since then. The summer of 2014 was the hottest the world had ever experienced since record keeping began in the 1880s.

But high temperatures are only part of the climate change picture. Extreme weather of all sorts has become more frequent. Scientists believe that climate change has been the cause of epic floods, withering droughts, giant wildfires, massive storms, and even intense cold spells in the first two decades of the twenty-first century.

Some governments, activists, and forward-looking researchers are exploring a wide range of conservation measures as well as developing alternative fuel sources, such as solar power and wind power. But so far, the increased use of alternative fuels has not led to a decreased use of petroleum. In fact, people use more petroleum each year, even as it becomes harder to get. Societies around the globe depend on industrialized, petroleum-based economies. How do we balance the pros and cons of petroleum on a planet that has only a limited natural supply? The struggles to address these complex issues are playing out on the world stage, with the future of the planet hanging in the balance.

CHAPTER TWO

THE AGE OF OIL

Much of the petroleum on Earth is far underground and under the seafloor, trapped beneath layers of rock. In some places, petroleum oozes up naturally to Earth's surface through cracks in rocks. Sometimes crude oil bubbles up. Sometimes thick, sticky bitumen comes to the surface. In the ancient world, humans took advantage of the naturally flowing resource for numerous uses. For example, more than forty thousand years ago, hunter-gatherers in ancient Syria used bitumen to attach stone blades to the shafts of spears and other tools. In ancient Mesopotamia, in what became Iraq, builders used bitumen as mortar between bricks, as waterproofing for boats and sewers, and as plaster for the walls of houses.

The ancient Byzantines, based in what became Turkey, mixed crude oil with quick lime, sulfur, and other ingredients to make a substance called Greek fire. When lit, Greek fire burned ferociously—even on water. In about 675 CE, at the

ΠΩρρικων·Ημαωδεκαιτοοκλαστωπρωπολουιπυρι

λοερωμαν πυρπολ ΤΟΝΤΩΝΕΝΑΗΤΓΘλΟΝ·

An illustration from the twelfth century depicts the use of Greek fire during a sea battle between the Byzantines and the Saracens in the sixth century CE. Developed by the Byzantines, Greek fire consisted of a flammable combination of crude oil, quicklime, sulfur, and other ingredients.

Battle of Cyzicus in Turkey, Byzantine sailors pumped Greek fire onto the ships of their Arab enemies. Other military forces poured Greek fire into clay or iron containers, which they hurled into enemy lines by hand or shot with catapults.

In North America, many American Indians used petroleum. As far back as 8000 BCE, the Chumash of what eventually became Southern California used asphalt from tar pits as caulking for their canoes, waterproofing for baskets and dishes, and glue for assembling tools and decorative objects. Members of the Iroquois Confederacy, an alliance of six tribes in what became the northeastern United States, used oil as an insect repellant and as salve for wounds. Starting in the fifteenth century, they dug pits along creeks to collect crude oil that seeped from the ground. For centuries, American Indian communities traded in petroleum. The Seneca, who belonged to the Iroquois Confederacy, did an especially brisk business extracting and trading crude oil from land that became Pennsylvania and New York.

Early European settlers in North America did not use petroleum in the same ways that Indians did. Some traveling salesmen and quack healers sold it as medicine, falsely billing it as a cure for a wide range of ailments. But until the nineteenth century, most white Americans saw petroleum as a nuisance that polluted their water supplies and interfered with farming and mining operations.

That outlook changed in the mid-1800s, when oil proved to be the solution for a pressing international problem.

LET THERE BE LIGHT

By then North Americans and Europeans were running out of their highest-quality lamp fuel: spermaceti, an oily substance that came from the heads of sperm whales. Spermaceti gave off a bright light when burned and, unlike many animal fats and plant oils commonly used as lamp fuel, didn't give off a foul smell. But during the nineteenth century, whales were hunted almost to extinction. With the spermaceti supply dwindling, Europeans and North Americans began looking for another lamp fuel that would burn equally well.

In 1849 Canadian geologist Abraham Gesner found that petroleum could be distilled into a flammable liquid that he called kerosene. Six years later, a group of US entrepreneurs hired Yale University chemist Benjamin Silliman Jr. to perfect the distillation process. Silliman developed a simple, inexpensive technique for refining crude oil to create kerosene.

Silliman's employers realized that kerosene could easily overtake spermaceti as the nation's best-selling lamp fuel. These men formed the Pennsylvania Rock Oil Company (later called the Seneca Oil Company) and began drilling for oil in northwestern Pennsylvania, where petroleum often bubbled up along riverbanks and onto farmland. In the town of Titusville in 1859, Pennsylvania Rock Oil Company drillers struck oil at 70 feet (21 m) below the ground. The discovery sparked an oil rush. Over the next decade, drilling operations sprang up throughout western Pennsylvania and in other oil-rich areas, including New York, Ohio, Kentucky,

In 1858 the Seneca Oil Company (originally the Pennsylvania Rock Oil Company) hired oil driller Edwin Drake *(foreground right)* to locate oil in Pennsylvania. In August 1859, Drake and his crew struck oil at 70 feet (21 meters).

and western Virginia (which became the state of West Virginia in 1863). And when drillers found oil, they often found natural gas at the same well. That gas could also be sold as lamp fuel.

Americans soon found a host of new uses for petroleum. Oil could be used to lubricate gears and wheels of large machines. It could be burned to create steam to power engines and turbines. With the Industrial Revolution under way, fuel was needed for steam-powered trains, ships, and machinery, as well as to power new factories operating across the United States and Europe.

One rapidly growing US industrial center—and a focal point for the new oil industry—was Cleveland, Ohio. During the 1860s, a young entrepreneur and Cleveland resident named John D. Rockefeller began to take an interest in petroleum. He wanted to invest in a safe, profitable business venture, and he saw the financial potential in oil. In 1870 he formed Standard Oil of Ohio, which opened large oil refineries in the eastern United States and soon became an industry giant.

European companies wanted a piece of the action too. At about this time, several European and Russian firms focused on central Asia, where they began developing a large oil field in Baku, in what later became Azerbaijan. The Royal Dutch Company located oil fields in Sumatra in Southeast Asia, an area then under Dutch control, and became a dominant force in providing oil worldwide. It was the beginning of a long tradition of companies crossing borders to stake claims on coveted oil fields.

HORSEPOWER

For a brief time, it seemed that the petroleum boom might not last. In the 1880s, Americans and Europeans began switching from kerosene and gas lamps to the newly invented electric lightbulb. Electric light was cleaner and brighter than lamplight, with no smells, smoke, or mess. Right on the heels of electric lighting, however, came the invention of the automobile in the 1880s. Cars ran on gasoline, and the petroleum industry was set to experience yet another surge.

Cars exploded in popularity. By 1900 eight thousand cars had been sold in the United States. The demand for petroleum was greater than ever, and oil companies searched for new supplies. In 1901 a consortium of drillers tapped an enormous oil field in eastern Texas. The increased oil supply brought down gasoline prices, which made operating a car more affordable. By 1912 more than nine hundred thousand cars were registered in the United States. And the numbers kept climbing, especially after manufacturer Henry Ford began producing affordable automobiles using the assembly line technique. As the number of cars increased, companies opened gas stations to serve motorists, who had previously bought gas at hardware stores, grocery stores, and other shops with limited supplies. Traffic lights, parking meters, and paved roads were not far behind.

BLOOD, SWEAT, AND PETROLEUM

In the 1890s, inventors adapted the internal combustion engine—designed originally for automobiles—for numerous other vehicles, such as tractors and trucks. By the early 1900s, navies were switching from coal-powered ship engines to those that ran on oil, which produced more energy per pound and was much easier than coal to store and transport. Oil was bigger than ever before, and the United States was at the forefront of the industry. The discovery of vast oil deposits in California and Texas at the turn of the twentieth century helped make the United States the world's top oil supplier. By 1909 US oil production had surpassed the combined production of all other countries in the world.

During World War I (1914–1918), fought mostly in Europe between a group of nations known as the Allied powers and a group called the Central powers, petroleum became a critical weapon. Armies employed gasoline-powered tanks, trucks, motorcycles, ambulances, and airplanes. The conflict eventually grew to involve the Middle East and the United States. After joining the war effort in 1917, the United States supplied the Allies with petroleum to fuel war vehicles. Their enemies, the Central powers (including Germany, Austria-Hungary, the Ottoman Empire, and Bulgaria), didn't have access to as much petroleum. With smaller domestic oil deposits and failed attempts to capture oil fields in Russia and Romania, the Central powers were at a distinct energy disadvantage. When the war was over, British foreign secretary George Curzon remarked that the Allies had "floated to victory upon a wave of oil."

Oil was bigger than ever before, and the United States was at the forefront of the industry.

As part of the negotiations that ended the war, France and Britain, took control of parts of the Middle East. By then vast oil fields had been found throughout the region. European and US oil companies established drilling operations across the Middle East. For example, Standard Oil of California (later called the Arabian American Oil Company, or Aramco) made a deal to explore for oil in the independent kingdom of Saudi Arabia. The company discovered a giant, profitable oil field there in 1938.

The next year, World War II (1939–1945) began in Europe, pitting Germany and its allies—known as the Axis powers—against France, Britain, and other nations, again known as the Allied powers. Almost immediately, Britain planned to disrupt Germany's petroleum industry, hoping to cripple the enemy's transportation systems. In an effort known as the Oil Campaign, Allied forces bombed numerous Axis-controlled oil refineries, oil pipelines, and ships and trains carrying oil to German troops.

The United States entered the war in December 1941 and helped the Allies escalate their attacks on German petroleum supplies. The United States also shared its plentiful oil supply with the British military,

TURN THAT GAS DOWN

This World War II–era poster from Great Britain encouraged civilians to save energy on the home front, freeing up more petroleum for use in the war effort.

ensuring that the Allies would have enough fuel. On the home front, the Allied governments rationed gasoline, limiting the amount that each family or business could buy so that more oil would be available for military uses.

The Allies' fuel advantage had concrete results on the battlefield. In one military operation, British forces defeated German general Erwin Rommel in Egypt in 1942, partly because his army ran out of oil and his resupply lines were damaged or disabled by the enemy. He lamented, "The bravest men can do nothing without guns, the guns nothing without plenty of ammunition, and neither guns nor ammunition are of much use in mobile warfare unless there are vehicles with sufficient petrol to haul them around."

DRIVE-IN

After the war ended with an Allied victory, the US economy boomed. Veterans returning to civilian life got married and started families, bought big shiny new cars, and moved to new suburban housing developments. Previously, Americans had relied heavily on public transportation—buses, streetcars, and trains. But after the war, as suburbs grew on the edges of big cities, car travel became the norm. Americans enjoyed drive-in movies, drive-in restaurants, and long-distance vacations with the whole family piled into a big sedan or station wagon. Most cars were gas guzzlers, running only about 15 miles (24 km) on 1 gallon (3.8 liters) of gas, but most drivers didn't mind, since gas was plentiful and cheap—thirty cents a gallon or less in 1950.

Auto travel became even easier once the United States began building the 41,000-mile (66,000 km) Interstate Highway System in 1956. Originally planned for national defense, so that US forces could travel quickly across the nation in wartime, wide interstate highways allowed cars and trucks to speed down the road, mile after mile, without stoplights or intersections to slow them down. As the interstate system spread across the nation, businesses such as roadside motels and restaurants cropped up along the roadway, with easy on- and off-ramps for quick access.

Other booming industries also relied on petroleum. Airplanes running on gasoline or jet fuel carried travelers across the country and across oceans. Scientists and engineers used petrochemicals to develop new plastics, fertilizers, paints, resins, and synthetic fibers. Many American homes switched from coal-based heating to central heating units powered by oil, gas, or petroleum-generated electricity.

To meet the ever-growing demand, oil companies continued to search for new sources of petroleum. The search led them offshore, under oceans and lakes. Drillers set up floating oil rigs in the Gulf of Mexico, the Pacific Ocean, the Persian Gulf, and other bodies of water. Despite the technological challenges of drilling deep underwater, offshore drilling flourished during the postwar decades, with operations in the Gulf of Mexico producing more than nine hundred thousand barrels of oil a day in 1968 alone.

DIRTY DEAL

Until the mid-1960s, automobile emissions in the United States were not regulated by the federal government. For every 10,000 miles (16,090 km) traveled, each mid-twentieth-century car spewed more than 2,000 pounds (907 kilograms) of hydrocarbons, carbon monoxide, nitrogen oxide, and lead into the atmosphere. This pollution took the form of gases, tiny droplets of liquid, and tiny solid particles. In Los Angeles, California, which had more freeways than any other city, a yellowish haze often hung in the air. The air pollution stung people's eyes and sometimes made breathing difficult. Angelenos called the haze smog, a mixture of the words *smoke* and *fog*.

BETTER LIVING THROUGH CHEMISTRY

The petrochemical industry exploded in the United States during World War II. The Allies desperately needed rubber to make tires for military vehicles, but war in the Pacific had cut off Allied access to Southeast Asian rubber plantations. The petroleum industry filled in the gap with synthetic rubber, made from the petrochemicals styrene and butadiene. The military also needed fabric to make parachutes, uniforms, and other materials. The petroleum industry supplied synthetic fibers such as nylon, also made from petrochemicals, to fill that need. The early petrochemical industry was based around Houston, Texas, an area with plentiful oil and gas, as well as easy access to ocean shipping through the Gulf of Mexico.

The industry continued to boom after the war, as scientists developed new petrochemical-based plastics, resins, fertilizers, paints, and fibers. Consumers eagerly bought new plastic and synthetic products, many of which were lighter, safer, stronger, cheaper, and easier to clean than the products they replaced. Plastic bottles, for instance, didn't shatter when dropped, as glass bottles could. Synthetic leather was cheaper than leather made from animal hide. Laminated plastic countertops wouldn't warp or stain like wooden countertops. Plastic wrap protected food from bacteria better than waxed paper did. Plastic garbage pails weighed less than metal ones and were much more difficult to dent.

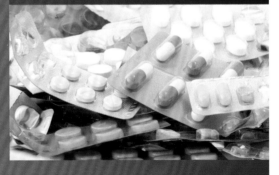

Petrochemicals are used in the manufacture of many pharmaceutical drugs, as well as their plastic packaging.

In the twenty-first century, the petrochemical industry spans the globe. Middle Eastern petrochemical companies are growing especially quickly, while the United States' plentiful supply of liquid natural gas—used almost exclusively in manufacturing petrochemicals—keeps it at the forefront of the business. Regardless of where they are manufactured, petrochemicals remain in high demand. They are used in an ever-widening range of products, from cosmetics to computers.

In the 1960s, to cut down on smog, California legislators passed several laws requiring pollution-control devices on cars in that state. The federal government followed suit, passing the Motor Vehicle Air Pollution Control Act of 1965 and the Air Quality Act of 1967. Engineers developed new pollution-control technology such as lead-free gasoline and catalytic converters. Catalytic converters turn harmful pollutants in car exhaust, such as nitrogen oxides and carbon monoxide, into harmless substances, such as water vapor, nitrogen, and oxygen.

But air pollution wasn't the only problem created by petroleum use. By the 1960s, vast amounts of oil were traveling through underground pipelines, overland in train cars, and across the oceans in ships. Thousands of rigs were drilling and pumping oil both on land and under the oceans. Accidents happened.

In January 1969, a blowout occurred at a Union Oil drilling platform in the Pacific Ocean, 6 miles (9.7 km) off the coast of Santa Barbara, California. Under great pressure from the earth below, oil began to spew uncontrollably from wells drilled into the ocean floor. Union Oil hadn't installed proper blowout preventers to control the oil in such a disaster. As the oil gushed upward, a giant oil slick spread across the surface of the Santa Barbara Channel. About 30 miles (48 km) of scenic California beaches were coated in a thick sludge of oil. Thousands of oil-soaked birds, elephant seals, sea lions, and other animals—dead or dying—washed up onshore as well. Before the gusher was plugged, more than 3 million gallons (11 million liters) of crude oil had spewed into the ocean. The cleanup took months and cost millions of dollars.

The oil spill—along with other environmental disasters, such as a fire caused by chemical spills in the Cuyahoga River in Cleveland—galvanized the nation and helped bolster a fledgling environmental movement. Following the spill, US president Richard M. Nixon authorized the creation of the Environmental Protection Agency (EPA) in 1972. With the launching of the

The oil spill—along with other environmental disasters, such as a fire caused by chemical spills in the Cuyahoga River in Cleveland—galvanized the nation and helped bolster a fledgling environmental movement.

EPA, Congress went on to pass a variety of laws intended to ensure clean air, clean water, and the protection of endangered species across the United States.

CONTROLLING THE SPIGOT

By then the United States had used up much of its domestic oil. Instead of selling petroleum to other countries, it had begun importing—relying heavily on oil shipments from Saudi Arabia. The focus of the oil rush had shifted from US soil to Middle Eastern countries with still-plentiful petroleum supplies. Five oil-rich nations—Iran, Iraq, Kuwait, Saudi Arabia, and Venezuela—had formed the Organization of the Petroleum Exporting Countries (OPEC) in 1960. Throughout the 1960s and 1970s the organization grew to include several other countries, mostly in the Middle East. Together the OPEC nations possessed more than 75 percent of the world's accessible oil reserves. Most of the oil companies operating in OPEC territory were foreign-owned. But OPEC was determined to change that.

In the 1970s, OPEC nations began nationalizing their oil industries—making them government-owned businesses. First, Saudi Arabia bought Aramco from its US owners and renamed it Saudi Aramco. Other OPEC members followed suit. They continued to supply oil to foreign countries, and in many cases, foreign companies—with their valuable expertise and technologies—still operated in OPEC territory. However, they did so under newly negotiated deals that redirected more profits to the nationalized oil companies and less to the foreign companies. These arrangements gave OPEC tremendous economic and political clout.

MIDEAST PETROPOLITICS

Oil frequently plays a decisive role in international politics, particularly in the Middle East, which has historically controlled the largest supplies of petroleum in the world. For example, in 1953 Iran's new prime minister nationalized the British-owned Anglo-Iranian Oil Company. Britain, upset by this move, turned to its ally the United States for help. The US Central Intelligence Agency (CIA), the nation's spy organization, orchestrated a coup, or overthrow of the government, in Iran. The United States then restored Iran's old leader, Mohammad Reza Pahlavi, to power. He was a harsh dictator, but he secured support from the United States and Britain by allowing the Anglo-Iranian Oil Company, as well as US oil companies, to continue to extract oil from Iran.

The Middle Eastern oil supply was threatened again in 1990, when Iraq invaded neighboring Kuwait and moved to invade Saudi Arabia. Both Kuwait and Saudi Arabia were major suppliers of oil to the United States. The United States wanted to help its Middle Eastern allies—and to protect its oil supply. The United States amassed a coalition of thirty-nine nations, which quickly defeated the Iraqi army.

US president George W. Bush *(left)* and Prince Abdullah of Saudi Arabia meet at Bush's home in Crawford, Texas, on April 25, 2002. The United States still maintains strong diplomatic ties with Saudi Arabia, the world's largest oil producer and exporter.

When President George W. Bush sent troops to Iraq again in 2003, many critics believed that the United States wanted to control Iraq's oil. Antiwar protesters held up signs that read "No Blood for Oil." President Bush and other US leaders denied a desire to obtain Iraqi oil, citing other reasons for the invasion. But shortly afterward, Iraqi oil, previously nationalized under Iraqi president Saddam Hussein, did start to flow to US oil companies. By August 2005, with the conflict still under way, more than 50 percent of Iraqi oil exports were being shipped to the United States.

OPEC used that clout after Israel, a Jewish state in the Middle East, defeated forces from neighboring Egypt, Jordan, and Syria in the Yom Kippur War (1973). The United States had provided military support to Israel, angering surrounding Middle Eastern nations. Following the war, several OPEC members, including Saudi Arabia, instituted an embargo. They directed oil companies operating in their nations to drastically cut oil shipments to the United States and other oil-dependent countries that supported Israel.

When the embargo began, Americans felt the effects almost immediately. With a shortage of oil, prices skyrocketed. Before the embargo, Americans could buy gas at thirty-eight cents a gallon. Six months later, gas cost eighty-four cents a gallon—a tough increase at a time when the minimum wage for US workers was only two dollars an hour. Because supplies were so low, many gas stations simply shut down. If a station did have gas, local drivers flocked there and waited in long lines that often snaked for miles down city streets. Often people reached the pumps after a long wait only to learn that the gas was sold out.

Due to limited supply
SORRY...
NO GASOLINE TODAY
OPEN for your other driving needs.

In 1973 the United States backed its ally Israel in the Yom Kippur War. Angered by this move, OPEC nations set up an oil embargo, cutting off shipments of oil to the United States. Gas prices shot up, lines at gas stations stretched for blocks, and pumps sometimes ran out entirely.

National leaders negotiated an end to the embargo in March 1974. But the United States realized it needed to make changes. President Richard Nixon spoke about making the nation more energy independent—with less reliance on foreign oil. By then the American-owned Atlantic Richfield Company had discovered a giant oil field at Prudhoe Bay in Alaska. In 1974 construction began on a pipeline to carry that oil to the port of Valdez, Alaska. Then it could be shipped to refineries in California and elsewhere. Also in 1974, to guard against future oil shortages, the US government created the Strategic Petroleum Reserve, a 727-million-barrel emergency oil supply stored in four sites off the Gulf of Mexico coast. Managed by the Department of Defense, the oil could be used, sold, or lent during national emergencies such as natural disasters or wars.

Spurred by the higher gasoline prices of the 1970s, many Americans traded in their gas guzzlers for more fuel-efficient cars. In 1975 Congress passed the first national fuel-efficiency standards for cars (but not for trucks or early-style sports utility vehicles). The law called for doubling average automobile fuel economy—from 13.5 miles (22 km) per gallon to 27.5 miles (44 km) per gallon—in ten years. The government also instituted a 55-mile (88.5 km) per hour speed limit on US highways. Cars burn less gas at lower speeds, so setting a limit improved fuel efficiency. (In 1995 the law was repealed and states were allowed to set their own speed limits.)

Interest in alternative fuels also grew. Engineers had been studying renewable energy since the 1950s, focusing on solar power and geothermal power (energy coming from the heat of Earth's interior) and hoping to find more efficient, less expensive ways to heat homes. The 1970s ushered in a surge of public enthusiasm for alternative energy sources. In 1974 the US Department of Energy launched the Solar Energy Research Institute to study the best way to harness power from the sun. President Jimmy Carter signed the Solar Photovoltaic

Energy Research Development and Demonstration Act of 1978 and had thirty-two solar panels—to run a water-heating system—installed on the roof of the White House in 1979. (Carter's successor, Ronald Reagan, had the system dismantled in 1986.) As part of the government's push for cleaner energy, the US National Aeronautics and Space Administration (NASA) built thirteen experimental wind turbines to improve wind-power technology. Local, state, and federal governments also invested in wind farms and solar power systems, as did private businesses. Companies also built nuclear power plants around the United States and elsewhere.

In the 1980s, gas consumption dropped to such an extent that oil-producing nations found themselves with more oil than they could sell. The surplus led to a sharp plunge in gas prices, which encouraged drivers to begin using more gas again. With oil once again readily available and cheap,

In 1979 President Jimmy Carter *(center)* showed off the White House's new solar hot water heating system to photographers and reporters. The panels were used to heat water for the First Family's residence.

broad pushes toward energy conservation and alternative energy lost much of their early momentum and public support.

CONTINUED DEPENDENCE, RISING COSTS

Oil spills also continued to plague the industry. In 1989 the American oil tanker *Exxon Valdez*, under command of a captain who had been drinking on the job, struck a reef in Alaska's Prince William Sound, an arm of the Pacific Ocean. The collision ruptured eight of the ship's eleven cargo tanks, allowing nearly 11 million gallons (41 million liters) of crude oil to spill into the water. Oil fouled 1,500 miles (2,400 km) of beaches along Prince William Sound. Deaths of animals—including birds, whales, and fish—numbered in the hundreds of thousands. The spill severely crippled the Alaskan fishing industry, causing more than $300 million in economic damage. Tourism, a major source of income for Alaskans, decreased by 35 percent in south western Alaska in the year after the spill. The cleanup cost $2.5 billion and took more than three years. The state of Alaska and the US government brought criminal and civil charges against Exxon, and thousands of individual Alaskans filed a class-action lawsuit against the company. The legal proceedings dragged out for more than twenty years. Ultimately Exxon paid more than $4 billion in fines, cleanup costs, and lawsuit settlements.

Meanwhile, petroleum was wreaking havoc on the global environment. Beginning in the 1970s, scientists noted a general rise in temperatures on Earth. Some believed the increase was linked to large amounts of carbon dioxide entering the atmosphere from the burning of fossil fuels. By the 1990s, scientists were warning that rising temperatures could lead to melting polar ice, rising sea levels, and more extreme weather on Earth. Environmentalists took note, and some people called for reductions in greenhouse gas emissions. Others doubted the warnings, suggesting that Earth's climate was not actually changing

In 1989, after the *Exxon Valdez* tanker spilled millions of gallons of crude oil into the waters off Alaska, men and women worked to clean beaches of Prince William Sound. Even decades after the disaster, environmental effects of the oil spill persist.

or that emissions were not responsible for the shifts.

Industry leaders balked at changing their practices to reduce greenhouse gas emissions, arguing that it would be too expensive. Factories and other businesses would have to invest in costly new pollution-control and alternative-fuel technology to reduce emissions. Industry leaders said that businesses and the entire economy would be hurt by such efforts—and that people would lose jobs in the resulting economic downturn.

"DRILL, BABY, DRILL."

By the beginning of the twenty-first century, petroleum's costs to society and to the global environment had become abundantly clear. Oil spills continued, and most scientists agreed that carbon emissions from the burning of petroleum and other fossil fuels had led to climate change. Political tensions in the Middle East frequently threatened to disrupt US access to important overseas oil, and when the supply was unreliable, gas prices rose. Hoping to reduce petroleum use, some American businesses began investing in alternative fuels such as ethanol (derived from plants) as well as in alternative power sources such as wind, solar, and geothermal energy.

But the need for oil remained great. And many Americans believed that petroleum itself was not the problem. The real problem, they said, was where and how the United States got its petroleum. Some analysts argued that it was time to stop relying so heavily on unpredictable and increasingly expensive oil shipments from abroad. Instead, these people contended, US companies should take advantage of new technologies to tap previously inaccessible petroleum reserves closer to home. Though the oil fields of the early American oil boom had long ago been exhausted, petroleum deposits still existed in the deepest waters of the Gulf of Mexico, the shale formations of North Dakota and other regions of the United States, and the Alberta tar sands of friendly neighboring Canada. Petroleum was also present in many American wilderness areas and offshore waters that had been legally declared off-limits to oil drilling to protect key natural resources, such as endangered plants and animals. Proponents of increased domestic oil production thought that drilling should be allowed in these protected areas. They noted that the petroleum industry provided jobs to many Americans and that increased oil drilling would reduce gas prices and help decrease US dependence on foreign oil.

The issue came front and center during the 2008 US presidential election. The Republican Party favored increased oil drilling on US lands and waters, and at Republican campaign rallies across the nation, "Drill, baby, drill" became a rallying cry. Democratic presidential candidate Barack Obama also acknowledged the appeal of drilling at home, stating, "We can and should increase our domestic production of oil and gas."

And indeed, drilling did increase after Obama won the election and took office in 2009. By 2014 the United States had surpassed Saudi Arabia as the world's top oil producer. And as many industry insiders had predicted, US dependence on foreign oil began to drop. Also in 2014, for the first time in more than thirty years, the United States began exporting some of its oil to other countries—a move that marked "a new era in US energy and [in] US energy relations with the rest of the world," according to energy historian Daniel Yergin. Some experts say that trend will only last until North America's remaining domestic oil supply peaks and then begins to run out around 2022. But whatever the long-term outlook, the United States has once again emerged as a major player in global petroleum politics.

CHAPTER THREE

BIG OIL

A common nickname for the oil industry is Big Oil—and that name is appropriate. Oil companies are among the largest businesses in the world. Consider just one US oil company, Chevron, which is headquartered in San Ramon, California, and works globally. In Africa, Chevron operates oil fields in Angola, Chad, Nigeria, and several other countries. In central Asia, Chevron extracts oil in Azerbaijan and Kazakhstan. Other Asian operations of Chevron are in Cambodia, China, Indonesia, and Thailand. Chevron has offshore oil rigs in Brazil and Venezuela in South America. Additional Chevron offshore operations are in the North Sea of western Europe. Chevron extracts oil from Canada's tar sands in Alberta. At home in the United States, Chevron extracts oil in ten states, plus the Gulf of Mexico. Chevron also owns oil refineries, pipelines, and gas stations in the United States and around the world. Chevron is financially powerful, with annual profits of about $26 billion.

This enormous oil company is far from the world's largest, however. In fact, Chevron is only the world's ninth-largest oil company. In 2012 it produced 3.5 million barrels of oil per day—well behind PetroChina, a government-owned Chinese company, No. 5 on the list with 4.4 million barrels per day. Exxon ranked fourth with 5.3 million barrels per day. In 2012 Saudi Aramco was the world's top producer, with 12.5 million barrels per day and profits of more than $40 billion per year.

Like Chevron, most big oil companies operate worldwide. And these giant companies often combine forces, making their operations even more substantial. For instance, in the first decade of the twenty-first century, Chevron partnered with ExxonMobil, Royal Dutch Shell, BP (formerly British Petroleum), and several Russian oil companies to build the Caspian Pipeline, which carries oil west from the Tengiz oil field in Kazakhstan to a port on the Black Sea. Such consortiums are commonplace in the oil industry. They enable big companies to share the cost of an expensive development project, to share the profits if an

A worker for PetroChina checks equipment at Moxi Natural Gas Purification Plant in southern China. PetroChina is the country's largest producer of oil.

An exploration rig searches for petroleum in the massive desert of Rub al-Khali, also known as the Empty Quarter. Stretching across parts of Saudi Arabia, Oman, Yemen, and the United Arab Emirates, the Empty Quarter is thought to contain the largest petroleum reserves on the planet.

investment pays off, and to split the losses if the project fails. Oil companies can't work on foreign soil without permission from the government in charge there, so national governments are often included in oil consortiums. For example, the government of Kazakhstan is a partner in the Caspian Pipeline project.

DEEP POCKETS

"If you don't spend, you're going to shrink," says Dan Pickering, president of an American-based investment bank that works with oil companies. To ensure future growth, oil companies invest billions of dollars each year in exploratory wells, drilling equipment, pipelines, and oil leases that permit them to drill in specific areas.

Companies also spend millions of dollars every year to support laws that protect the interests of their businesses and to fight those that don't. One such effort played out in California in 2006. That year Californians were scheduled to vote on a law called Proposition 87 (or Prop 87). If passed, the law would have placed a 1.5 to 6 percent tax on each barrel of oil drilled in the state. The tax was expected to generate about $400 million per year for California over a ten-year period. The money was slated for investment in clean, renewable energy, such as solar and wind power. Other oil-producing states impose a similar tax, and more than 60 percent of Californians thought Proposition 87 was a good idea when it was first introduced.

But the companies that pump most of the oil in California—Chevron, ExxonMobil, Royal Dutch Shell, and Occidental—vigorously opposed the law. If Prop 87 passed, the tax would cut into their profits. So the oil companies spent $100 million to convince voters that Prop 87 was a bad idea. The companies hired

SEARCH TECHNOLOGY

To search for oil, geologists start with simple observations. They study photographs of Earth's surface taken from airplanes and satellites. Certain land formations indicate that oil might be located belowground. For instance, a bulge on an otherwise flat surface is sometimes an indication of oil trapped below.

Other methods are more high-tech. The most important of these is seismic exploration. Seismic waves are vibrations that travel underground. The waves interact differently with different types of rock. For instance, seismic waves behave one way when moving through dense rocks and another way when moving through porous, oil-filled rocks. Scientists use specialized trucks on land and air guns underwater to create seismic waves. Other devices analyze the waves as they travel. This analysis tells scientists when waves are moving through rocks that might contain oil.

Once geologists have located a likely spot to dig for oil, they drill test wells. They pull up cores, or cylindrical samples of underground layers of rock. They study the cores to determine whether any rock layers contain oil and gas. If so, they can then determine the type of oil or gas, how extensive the deposit is, and how far underground it is.

After the data is collected, geologists use computers to create maps and models of the underground formations. These images help oil companies decide whether to develop the site and how to approach the project.

public relations firms to spread their message through ads. They gave money to business associations and political groups that shared their views. They paid for spokespeople to criticize the law on radio and TV shows and at public meetings. The spokespeople warned voters that if Prop 87 were enacted, oil companies would pass on their increased costs to consumers, driving up the price of gas. They even warned that oil companies might choose to leave California—and take thousands of oil industry jobs elsewhere—because it would cost too much to operate in the state.

On the other side of the debate, supporters of Prop 87 ran ads, held meetings, and put speakers on TV and radio. They sent the message that Prop 87 would help protect California's air, water, and wildlife—and noted that the cost to oil companies would be tiny in comparison to enormous oil company profits. But Big Oil had much more money to spend than the Prop 87 backers. "If we ran one TV ad, they ran two and a radio ad and a newspaper ad," said Yusef Robb, communications director for the pro-Prop 87 campaign. The Big Oil media blitz paid off. When Election Day rolled around, 55 percent of Californians voted no on Prop 87.

PLAYING POLITICS

The Prop 87 story is just one of many instances of Big Oil flexing its political and financial muscle. At the local, state, federal, and international levels, oil companies—like other major industries—are heavily involved in politics. In the United States, oil companies want legislation to open up more federally owned lands and more offshore waters to drilling for oil and gas. They support less strict environmental regulations, which would make drilling cheaper, easier, and less time-consuming. They also want to maximize their profits through tax breaks and lower royalty payments to federal and state governments. To achieve their goals, oil companies give large campaign contributions to political candidates and hire lobbying firms, all to influence lawmakers to support the Big Oil agenda.

In the 2000 presidential election, for example, Big Oil contributed handsomely to George W. Bush's campaign. Bush had been an oil executive in Texas early in his career and was friendly to the interests of the industry. His vice presidential running mate, Dick Cheney, had been in charge of Halliburton, a corporation that builds and operates oil refineries, oil pipelines, and other oil-related infrastructure. Once in office, Bush placed other oil-industry insiders in key positions throughout his administration. For example, he put the US Department of the Interior—the federal agency charged with protecting US national parks, wildlife refuges, and other public lands—under the control of Gale Norton, who had built a career as a lawyer and lobbyist representing the oil industry.

Bush put the US Department of the Interior—the federal agency charged with protecting US national parks, wildlife refuges, and other public lands—under the control of Gale Norton, who had built a career as a lawyer and lobbyist representing the oil industry.

As expected, the Bush administration backed laws favorable to Big Oil. Under Norton's leadership, the Department of the Interior reduced spending on the enforcement of environmental protection laws, allowed oil drilling in deep waters of the Gulf of Mexico, and opened up millions of acres of previously off-limits public land and water to both oil and gas drilling. Such actions drew heavy criticism from environmentalists. The Sierra Club, for example, called Norton "The Fox in Her Henhouse"—implying that Norton had plundered the very resource she had been hired to protect. But others praised Norton's work. Industrial Energy Consumers of America, a lobbying group for manufacturers, said her actions as interior secretary had helped the US economy. Getting more gas and oil to market would keep prices down, prevent job losses, and prevent manufacturing plant shutdowns, the organization said.

DEFENDING BIG OIL

When Exxon announced that it had earned $10.7 billion in profits in the first quarter of 2011—an increase of 69 percent over the same period in 2010—the news set off a firestorm. The US economy was in the middle of the Great Recession, a major economic slump. Many Americans were struggling to find work and pay their bills. At the time, gasoline cost almost four dollars a gallon—more than one dollar a gallon higher than the year before—adding to financial hardships for working people.

Many Americans felt that Exxon was exploiting consumers at the pump. As Nate Hagens of the Post Carbon Institute explained, "Americans are upset because they envision such hefty profits as direct transfers from their thin pocketbooks to Exxon."

President Barack Obama reacted to the news of Exxon's profits by calling for new taxes on the oil industry. Democratic congresswoman Nancy Pelosi of California said that existing tax breaks for oil companies should be reduced. Pelosi argued that tax breaks amounted to a handout to Exxon from US citizens—and that Exxon certainly didn't need a handout.

Exxon and other oil companies were quick to defend themselves. Industry leaders pointed out that many factors influence the price of gasoline and other petroleum products—and that these factors were often out of oil companies' control. For instance, political unrest in the Middle East sometimes disrupts the global oil supply, and when less oil is available on world markets, prices rise. Natural disasters can also interfere with the world's oil supply. For example, in the summer of 2005, Hurricane Katrina and Hurricane Rita damaged many oil drilling rigs and oil refineries on the Gulf Coast of the United States. A spike in oil prices followed these storms.

BIDDER 70: TIM DECHRISTOPHER

In December 2008, in the waning days of the administration of President George W. Bush, University of Utah student Tim DeChristopher learned that the US Bureau of Land Management (BLM), part of the US Department of the Interior, would be auctioning off thousands of acres of public land in Utah for oil and gas development. DeChristopher, a budding climate activist, headed to the auction in Salt Lake City, planning to make a protest.

But when he got to the auction, his tactics changed. On the spur of the moment, he registered as a bidder and began to bid on parcels of land, forcing up prices for the energy companies that were also bidding. Then, after almost half the parcels had been sold to energy companies, DeChristopher bid even higher, making winning bids on thirteen parcels. It soon became clear that he had no intention of actually buying the land and no money to pay for it, and he was kicked out of the auction.

DeChristopher's disruption of the auction temporarily kept certain lands out of the hands of energy companies, and in early 2009, Ken Salazar, secretary of the interior with the incoming Obama administration, voided the Utah auction altogether. Salazar determined that the BLM had violated federal rules in auctioning off the lands for energy development in the first place.

Nevertheless, DeChristopher had broken the law. He was convicted on felony charges and sentenced to two years in prison. Before and after his prison term, he toured the United States, speaking about the fight to protect Earth and to prevent climate change. He cofounded the environmental group Peaceful Uprising and has become a hero in the environmental movement.

Climate activist Tim DeChristopher speaks at a protest in front of the US Capitol Building in 2014, one year after serving a prison sentence.

As for oil industry profits, industry leaders argue that they are good for the US economy. "The U.S. oil and natural gas industry's strong earnings signal growing strength in our economy," said Jack Gerard, head of the American Petroleum Institute. Wrote economist Don Boudreaux, "When Exxon or Chevron has a good year, their larger-than-usual profits are often invested in new projects that grow the economy. The money is used to hire new employees, buy new goods and services from other businesses, research and develop new sources of energy and give raises to current employees."

Gerard and Boudreaux also noted that many pension funds—which provide income to people after they retire—are invested in oil company stocks. So when oil companies make big profits, many retirees and other Americans benefit. Industry leaders also argued against higher taxes on oil companies, saying that high taxes make it expensive for oil companies to do business in the United States and may lead them to move operations to other nations.

Hagens also stressed the importance of petroleum in modern life, observing, "[Oil companies] may not be noble, or admirable, or even likeable, but oil companies are providing a critical service to society. . . . Though gasoline is expensive relative to what we have become accustomed to, it is still incredibly cheap [considering] what it can accomplish for us."

MORE

No matter the outcomes of these ongoing controversies, chances are good that Big Oil will keep getting bigger—because global consumers continue to use more oil: 87.8 million barrels per day in 2010, 88.8 million barrels per day in 2011, 89.7 million barrels per day in 2012, and 90.3 million barrels per day in 2013. And demand for oil will continue to grow, unless and until major shifts in the world economy and energy technology

According to the American Petroleum Institute, the United States contains more than 190,000 miles (300,775 km) of liquid petroleum pipelines. The map below shows major crude oil pipelines in the United States and Canada as of 2014. Most of these pipelines run underground, carrying crude oil from onshore and offshore oil fields to refineries. Other pipelines (not shown here) then carry refined petroleum from refineries to storage depots (where the refined petroleum is loaded onto trucks for delivery to retail outlets). In addition, an extensive network of pipelines is dedicated to carrying non-liquid natural gas throughout the country. Canada is the United States' largest supplier of oil, with Canadian companies such as Enbridge, Kinder Morgan, and TransCanada transporting around 3 million barrels into the United States per day.

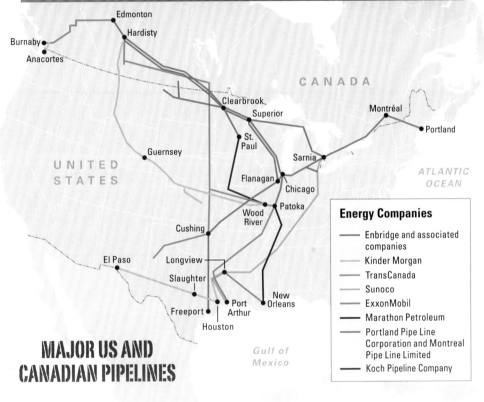

MAJOR US AND CANADIAN PIPELINES

Energy Companies

— Enbridge and associated companies
— Kinder Morgan
— TransCanada
— Sunoco
— ExxonMobil
— Marathon Petroleum
— Portland Pipe Line Corporation and Montreal Pipe Line Limited
— Koch Pipeline Company

occur. Former Chevron executive Don Paul sums up the reality of living in a petroleum-dependent world: "In the future, you are going to need every molecule of oil that you can get from every source."

CHAPTER FOUR
DAMAGES

In April 2010, the BP-operated oil rig _Deepwater Horizon_— as tall as a forty-story building—was in the Gulf of Mexico, about 40 miles (64 km) southeast of New Orleans, Louisiana. The rig's 126 workers had been building a well to tap an undersea petroleum deposit. The difficult job involved sending a set of telescoping pipes 5,000 feet (1,524 m) below the surface of the Gulf and then an additional 13,000 feet (3,962 meters) through the seabed to reach the bottom of the well.

On the evening of April 20, with construction on the well nearly complete, something went wrong. Without warning, a stream of hot, pressurized gas came rushing up the well from the seafloor. The well was equipped with a cement lining, provided by Halliburton, that was supposed to control the gas, but the cement mixture hadn't been prepared properly and wasn't strong enough to contain the rush of gas. The rig was also equipped with a blowout preventer, but it too failed.

Fire boats battle the blaze on the offshore oil rig *Deepwater Horizon* on April 21, 2010. Coast Guard helicopters, planes, and ships arrived for the rescue effort.

The stream of gas set off an explosion, engulfing the ship in a dramatic fireball. Eleven workers died. The *Deepwater Horizon* burned for two days and then sank.

Immediately after the explosion, at the bottom of the Gulf, from the opening of a broken pipe, oil came gushing out into the deep water. Engineers are skilled at plugging leaks at shallow-water oil rigs, which operate less than 500 feet (152 m) underwater. At that depth, divers can easily make repairs and inspections. But this well was leaking 5,000 feet (1,524 m) beneath the water's surface. Divers couldn't reach it. Engineers could work only with remotely controlled vehicles. Using such vehicles, BP and the US Coast Guard examined the leaking well. They declared that the leak was minor—just one thousand barrels of oil per day.

Within a week, a giant coating of oil had formed on the surface of the Gulf. People along the Gulf Coast watched and waited anxiously. Many of them made their living by fishing in the Gulf. They worried that oil would sicken and kill the fish and devastate the fishing economy.

As BP tried to figure out how to stop the spill, estimates of the amount of oil coming from the disabled well rose higher. On April 28, the US government upped the number to five thousand barrels per day. Soon Gulf Coast residents began spotting an oily film along coastal islands and wetlands. The region started to reek of oil. Residents complained of headaches, dizziness, burning eyes, and nausea. Concerned that seafood from the Gulf would be unsafe to eat, the federal government closed certain fishing areas.

In mid-May, an engineering professor from Purdue University in Indiana studied underwater video footage of oil flowing out of the well. He concluded that between fifty-six thousand and eighty-four thousand barrels of oil were flowing out of the well each day—up to sixteen times more than the government estimate. Underwater, the oil took the form of giant plumes—up to several miles wide and hundreds of feet thick.

To stop the leak, BP lowered a 74-ton (67-metric-ton) concrete-and-steel box over the broken well. The box was designed to capture the gushing oil and funnel it up to nearby tankers, but it quickly clogged up with gas and ice in the deep, frigid waters and wouldn't stay put on the seafloor. BP next tried shooting a stream of heavy fluid into the well to block the flow of oil, but the fluid was no match for the powerful force of the oil surging upward.

On the coast, dead, oil-soaked dolphins, turtles, and seabirds began to wash up onto beaches. The federal government closed more fishing waters and also declared a moratorium, or temporary ban, on deepwater drilling. Tourists who had planned to vacation on the normally clean, white Gulf Coast beaches canceled their reservations.

The oil kept flowing. It wasn't stopped until mid-July, when BP was finally able to fit a cap over the broken well. By August 5, the well had been sealed with tons of cement. The immediate crisis was over. But the effects of the disaster would linger for months and years. Some residents had been sickened by fumes from oil. Some tourist businesses and fishing operations had gone broke. And even after the beaches were cleaned, tourists returned, and life began to seem normal again, many questions remained. Was fish from the Gulf safe to eat? The US government said it was, and fishers returned to work. But studies showed that some fish and other sea life had been poisoned by petroleum. It would take years of research before scientists knew the full effects of the oil on the ecology of the Gulf Coast.

In September 2013, sixty-two deepwater rigs were operating in the Gulf—twice as many as three years earlier.

Few people wanted—or felt they could afford—to wait that long to find out. Oil industry leaders had invested billions of dollars in oil rigs and drilling equipment in the Gulf. They didn't want that machinery sitting idle when it could be earning revenue. In October 2010, President Obama lifted the moratorium on oil drilling in the Gulf, with new safety rules in place. By 2013 deepwater drilling was again booming in the Gulf of Mexico. In September of that year, sixty-two deepwater rigs were operating in the Gulf—twice as many as three years earlier.

DRIPPING AND GUSHING

The *Deepwater Horizon* disaster was the second-largest oil spill in history. The largest occurred during the Persian Gulf War (1990–1991), when Iraqi forces deliberately dumped hundreds of millions of gallons of oil into the Persian Gulf, hoping to prevent US troops from landing in Kuwait. But thousands of other spills, large and small, have occurred since large-scale oil drilling began in the 1850s. Each year millions of gallons of oil spill from tanker ships, wells, offshore rigs, pipelines, storage tanks, and trains.

Spills are a danger even at inactive drilling sites. In the Gulf of Mexico, since oil drilling began there in the 1940s, more than twenty-seven thousand oil and gas wells have been drilled and then shut down and plugged with cement after most of the oil was pumped. The cement on many old wells has deteriorated, however, allowing oil to seep up from the seafloor. The US government and individual states have resealed some wells, but experts believe that thousands of wells are leaking, with no comprehensive government plan for monitoring or repairing them.

Deteriorating cement was also to blame for an oil spill in April 2014 in the Chinese city of Lanzhou. Oil leaked from a corroded cement pipeline and contaminated the city water supply with the cancer-causing chemical benzene. Officials shut off water to one part of the city and warned other residents not to drink tap water for twenty-four hours. A few days later, city officials said that the water was again safe to drink, but many residents were skeptical. "The water still has a strange smell," said one city worker. "I won't drink it. I won't even touch it." Residents rushed to purchase bottled water, while workers replaced the old cement pipeline, in use since the 1950s, with a new cast-iron pipe, built to resist corrosion and even to withstand earthquakes.

BLACK DEATH

As the oil business grows around the world, the danger of oil disasters increases. For example, much of North America's oil travels cross-country by train. In 2013 about four hundred thousand train-car loads of petroleum moved across the United States, up from ninety-five hundred train-car loads in 2008. Most of the oil travels in tanks designed to hold nonflammable liquids—not flammable petroleum. The tanks can easily puncture in a crash, and in several train accidents, petroleum has burst into flames. In July 2013, for instance, a train carrying petroleum derailed and exploded in the center of a town in Québec,

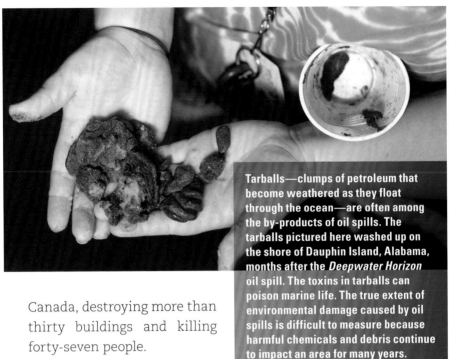

Tarballs—clumps of petroleum that become weathered as they float through the ocean—are often among the by-products of oil spills. The tarballs pictured here washed up on the shore of Dauphin Island, Alabama, months after the *Deepwater Horizon* oil spill. The toxins in tarballs can poison marine life. The true extent of environmental damage caused by oil spills is difficult to measure because harmful chemicals and debris continue to impact an area for many years.

Canada, destroying more than thirty buildings and killing forty-seven people.

Even when it's not burning, petroleum can be deadly. Breathing petroleum fumes can irritate the eyes and lungs. Touching petroleum—be it gasoline, crude oil, or clumps called tarballs that wash up on a beach—can cause itching, burning, and rashes. In large amounts, petroleum exposure can damage the lungs, nervous system, liver, and kidneys. The benzene found in gasoline is known to cause cancer.

After an oil spill, petroleum often contaminates water and soil. Wildlife is particularly vulnerable to petroleum exposure. Many animals die soon after swimming through an oil slick. They try to clean their bodies by grooming themselves, and in the process ingest poisonous oil. Others die more slowly after drinking water or eating plants or smaller animals contaminated by petroleum. Petroleum can also damage and kill fish eggs and larvae. Years after the 1989 *Exxon Valdez* spill, scientists discovered deformed and genetically damaged fish and animals in Prince William Sound. Oil had worked its way into the food chain. For instance, sea otters had eaten contaminated shellfish and then gotten sick themselves. An April 2010 study showed that more than twenty years after the spill, harlequin ducks were still ingesting oil from the *Exxon Valdez* spill.

The damage to wildlife from the *Deepwater Horizon* spill is hard to calculate, scientists say, because most of the animals killed by oil have not washed up on Gulf Coast beaches but have been carried to the Atlantic Ocean by sea currents. In 2014, using data on the numbers of dead birds found and using computer models of winds and ocean currents, two researchers

PROBLEMS WITH PLASTIC

Long after it has been extracted, petroleum continues to pose dangers to the environment and to human health. Products created from petroleum have proved to be as hazardous as they are indispensable. Plastics are a prime example.

Plastic is everywhere—including in the water. Every ocean in the world is polluted with plastic, as are numerous lakes, rivers, and streams. The building blocks of plastic products, tiny plastic pellets called nurdles, sometimes spill from shipping and storage containers during transit or at factories. Hundreds of millions of nurdles float in the oceans or wash up onshore. Finished plastic products make their way into waterways too. For instance, many soaps and facial scrubs contain tiny plastic beads that help rub off dead skin. After people use the scrubs, these microbeads travel with wastewater down sink drains, through sewers, and into sewage treatment plants. Because the beads are so tiny, they pass through filters at treatment plants and are discharged into waterways with treated water.

Larger plastic products also cause damage. A plastic bottle or bag, thoughtlessly tossed on the side of the road, might blow in the wind until it hits a body of water. In some places, ocean currents bring individual plastic pieces together into big eddies of "plastic soup." Seabirds, fishes, and other aquatic life frequently become entangled in plastic bags, strands, and packaging that has floated out to sea.

estimated that as many as eight hundred thousand birds had died in coastal and offshore waters as a result of the *Deepwater Horizon* spill.

Conscientious companies try to clean up after an oil spill. When the *Deepwater Horizon* spill began, BP sprayed chemical dispersants toward the leaking well. The dispersants dissolved some of the oil, breaking it into tiny droplets that mixed with seawater. Later BP worked with the US Coast Guard to contain, collect, and remove the spilled oil. The company hired workers to skim oil from the water and to shovel it off beaches.

Over time, wind, waves, and sunlight break down even the largest pieces of plastic into tiny particles. A 2014 study found that each square kilometer (0.4 square miles) of Lake Michigan contains about seventeen thousand tiny bits of plastic. These particles can be deadly to animals that live in or near water. Some animals unknowingly ingest bits of plastic with their nutrients. Others mistake bits of plastic for fish eggs, a food source, and eat them deliberately. Either way, these animals poison themselves with petrochemicals.

Plastic bottles and other waste collect in New Caledonia, an island nation under French rule located in the South Pacific Ocean east of Australia.

Plastic presents risks to humans as well. Scientists have linked phthalates, petrochemicals that make plastic products more flexible, to birth defects, cancer, and reproductive problems. Bisphenol A (BPA), a chemical used to harden plastic during the manufacturing process, causes similar health problems. Phthalates, BPA, and other petrochemicals can leach from plastics during dishwashing, heating, and handling. They can end up on human skin, in water, and in food. According to the US Centers for Disease Control and Prevention, 93 percent of Americans over the age of six have BPA in their urine. Some companies have stopped using BPA to make plastic, but the chemicals that have replaced it might be just as dangerous, scientists say.

That oil was carted to landfills. Workers also burned some of the oil, setting more than three hundred fires at sea. These cleanup methods earned BP and the Coast Guard widespread criticism, however, since fires at sea polluted the air and water, and the dispersants are also poisonous to plants and animals.

BP also relied on Mother Nature to help. At the bottom of the ocean, certain microorganisms consume oil. These are thought to have naturally cleaned up a large portion of the *Deepwater Horizon* spill. But most known oil-eating bacteria do not consume petroleum's most dangerous components: polycyclic aromatic hydrocarbons (PAHs). Without a human cleanup, these cancer-causing substances remain on the ocean floor.

Ultimately, even a multibillion-dollar effort (BP spent more than $14 billion on the cleanup) cannot completely clean an area after an oil spill. According to the National Wildlife Federation, three years after the *Deepwater Horizon* spill, nearly one-fifth of the leaked oil remained in the Gulf. Tarballs and mats of oil continued to wash up on Gulf Coast beaches regularly and are expected to do so for many more years.

WHO'S MINDING THE STORE?

After the *Deepwater Horizon* spill, a government investigation revealed the BP had cut corners in building its wells to save money and time—to get more oil to market less expensively. Halliburton, which had supplied the cement that lined the well, was also blamed: investigators discovered that Halliburton had known ahead of time that the cement used inside the well was substandard. The negligence of these big companies had led to the blowout on the rig, the deaths of eleven men, and billions of dollars in damage to the Gulf Coast. In 2013 BP pleaded guilty to 14 criminal charges related to the accident and agreed to pay $4 billion in penalties. The federal government also sued BP for an additional $13.7 billion. This civil lawsuit was ongoing as of January 2015.

At the time of the *Deepwater Horizon* spill, the Minerals Management Service (MMS) oversaw offshore oil drilling in the United States. In 2010 the MMS had just sixty safety inspectors to monitor about four thousand shallow and deepwater oil rigs in the Gulf of Mexico. Critics say that in addition to being under-staffed, oversight agencies such as MMS often operate as tools of Big Oil. Under political pressure from indus-try lobbyists, they expedite paper-work, rubber-stamp drilling applica-tions, and skimp on environmental and safety inspections.

The *New York Times* reported during the spill that MMS "routinely overruled its staff biologists and engineers who raised concerns about the safety and the environmental impact of certain drilling pro-posals in the gulf and in Alaska.... Scientists said they were also regularly pressured by agency officials to change the find-ings of their internal studies if they predicted that an accident was likely to occur or if wildlife might be harmed." Kierán Suck-ling of the Arizona-based Center for Biological Diversity charged, "MMS has given up any pretense of regulating the offshore oil industry. The agency seems to think its mission is to help the oil industry evade environmental laws."

The agency later acknowledged, "MMS—with its conflicting missions of promoting resource development, enforcing safety regulations, and maximizing revenues from offshore opera-tions and lack of resources—could not keep pace with the chal-lenges of overseeing industry operating in U.S. waters." In hopes

> "MMS—with its conflicting missions of promoting resource development, enforcing safety regulations, and maximizing revenues from offshore operations and lack of resources—could not keep pace with the challenges of overseeing industry operating in U.S. waters."
>
> —Minerals Management Service (MMS)

of preventing future drilling disasters, the federal government tightened safety rules and regulations for offshore drilling and divided MMS into three separate agencies, "with clear missions and additional resources necessary to fulfill those missions."

Even with stricter oversight, the petroleum industry remains dirty and dangerous. Oil workers, using heavy machinery and handling toxic chemicals, frequently suffer broken bones, burns, and even amputated limbs on the job. According to the US Bureau of Labor Statistics, 663 oil field workers were killed on the job between 2007 and 2012. According to the US Department of Labor, the fatality rate in the industry is seven times greater than the average rate for other US industries. The US Occupational Safety and Health Administration (OSHA) is in charge of worker safety, not just in the oil industry but in every other US industry. Like the MMS, it is understaffed and underfunded. Its monetary penalties for safety violations often amount to slaps on the wrist for large, profitable oil companies. And critics say that companies themselves are to blame—that they often use outdated equipment, skimp on worker training, and deliberately flout OSHA rules at job sites.

It's not just workers who pay the price. Nearly 150 oil refineries operate in the United States. These refineries, many of them old and using outdated equipment, release a variety of air pollutants, including benzene. One of the dirtiest refineries in the United States is Chevron Richmond Refinery, which sprawls across 3,000 acres (1,214 hectares) northeast of San Francisco, California. The nearly 120-year-old refinery abuts a large, low-income neighborhood, populated mostly by African American residents. Over the past few decades, people in Richmond have endured the refinery's many chemical spills, fires, leaks, explosions, and accidental releases of toxic gas. Efforts to clean up the facility and impose higher taxes on Chevron have faced tough pushback from the oil company. "Chevron has bought elections in this town for years," Richmond mayor Gayle McLaughlin said in 2007. She added, "I may be the mayor, but in this city, Chevron has the power."

OVERSEAS REGULATIONS

US environmental regulations are not nearly as tough or as strictly enforced as some critics would like. But in many countries, regulations are far weaker. In some places, oil drilling has turned vast areas into near toxic waste zones. One of the most extreme examples is the oil-rich African nation of Nigeria, where Royal Dutch Shell, PetroChina, and other international companies have been extracting oil for many years. According to Amnesty International (AI), a human rights organization, an estimated 1.5 million tons (1.4 million metric tons) of oil have spilled into the Niger delta, the area where the Niger River meets the Atlantic Ocean, over the last fifty years. This equals about one *Exxon Valdez* spill per year. The spills have killed birds, fish, and other wildlife; devastated fishing communities; damaged farmland; polluted water that people need for drinking, bathing, and cooking; and released dangerous fumes into the air. Cleanup efforts have been minimal. Critics blame many spills on old, corroded, and poorly maintained pipelines. Exacerbating the problem, poverty and anger at oil companies have led some Nigerians to vandalize and steal oil from pipelines.

Oil spills are only part of the problem in Nigeria. Natural gas is a by-product of oil drilling. In many drilling operations around the world, the gas is processed and used for energy. But in Nigeria, companies generally burn the gas as it comes out of oil wells, a process known as gas flaring. The burning gas contains benzene and other toxic chemicals. After drifting in the air, toxic soot from gas flaring settles back onto farms and waterways. The Nigerian government banned gas flaring in 1984 and fines companies that violate the ban. But the practice continues anyway because the financial penalties for flaring are very low. It's cheaper for oil companies to simply pay the fines than to invest in the necessary equipment to convert the natural gas into usable energy for homes and businesses.

Extraction has caused environmental disaster in oil-rich Latin America as well. In the 1970s, for instance, Texaco began drilling in the remote area of Lago Agrio, Ecuador. The nation had no strict environmental regulations at the time. During oil drilling, wells bring up large amounts of oily water, mixed with heavy metals from the soil. Standard practice in the United States and elsewhere is to reinject this "produced water" deep underground, into sealed wells. But in Ecuador, Texaco cut corners. It simply dumped the produced water into hundreds of above-ground pits. Locals charge that the toxic water has led to cancer deaths, miscarriages, and birth defects in humans, in addition to deaths of fish and livestock. Texaco and Chevron (which purchased Texaco in 2001) have been embroiled in lawsuits—both in Ecuador and in the United States—with Ecuadorian villagers for nearly twenty years. In 2011 an Ecuadorian judge ruled that Chevron was responsible for the contamination and ordered it

A woman dries cassava root, used in making tapioca, next to a gas flare fire in Warri, Nigeria. The practice of gas flaring is illegal but still common in Nigeria. Fumes and residue, known as toxic soot, are harmful to surrounding residents and environment.

to pay $18 billion in damages. The Ecuadorian supreme court cut the payment down by almost half—to $9.5 billion—in 2013. Chevron is unlikely to pay any amount, however. It argues that Texaco provided all the required site cleanup prior to its 2001 purchase by Chevron. In March 2014, a US court also ruled in favor of Chevron, stating that the lead lawyer for the Ecuadorian villagers had committed fraud and other crimes in pursuing the Ecuadorian verdict.

AN ONGOING GAMBLE

Oil companies emphasize their commitment to learning from their mistakes and preventing future spills. Bob Dudley, who took over as chief executive at BP after the *Deepwater Horizon* disaster, stressed in 2013, "After the accident . . . [w]e put in place structures and systems to further embed safety and operational reliability." He called safety the company's top priority and noted "decreases in losses of primary containment"—fewer oil leaks from BP operations—in 2012. Yet the oil industry remains a dangerous one. Dudley acknowledged that in 2012, "we did suffer four fatalities in our operations, two in vehicle accidents in the United Kingdom and Brazil, one resulting from a fall in India, and the other from a compressor station incident in the US."

Even with tougher safety regulations in place, experts warn that the risk of more oil industry accidents remains high—especially in previously unexplored areas, where new extraction technologies and unpredictable environmental conditions can increase the chances that something will go wrong. As the United States expands its petroleum operations into new territory, the appeal of a profitable domestic oil supply goes hand in hand with the threat of another disaster.

CHAPTER FIVE

PUSHING BOUNDARIES

In 2006 a representative of Houston-based Cabot Oil & Gas visited the home of Ron and Jeannie Carter, who lived on 75 acres (30 hectares) in the Endless Mountains of northeastern Pennsylvania. The man made the Carters an attractive offer: his company would pay them twenty-five dollars per acre (0.4 hectares) for the right to drill for natural gas on their land. And if Cabot found gas, the Carters would receive a big payout: 12.5 percent of the value of any gas that was extracted. That deal looked good to the Carters, retirees with a limited income. In earlier times, their family had farmed the land where they lived, but by 2006, it sat unused. After thinking it over, the Carters signed the agreement with Cabot. Many of their neighbors around Carter Road signed similar agreements.

The Endless Mountains sit on top of a formation called the Marcellus Shale, which stretches about a mile (1.6 km) underground from West Virginia in a northeasterly direction through eastern Ohio, most of Pennsylvania, and up to southern New York. The shale is filled with natural gas—500 trillion cubic feet (14 trillion cu. m) of gas by some calculations. In addition to the Marcellus, the United States has numerous shale gas formations including the Barnett Shale in Texas, the Mancos in Wyoming and Colorado, and the Antrim in Michigan.

Energy companies want this gas, and with the help of new technology, they are able to get it. Hydraulic fracturing, or fracking—which breaks the shale with streams of high-pressure fluids—has revolutionized drilling operations in rural areas across Pennsylvania and elsewhere. Oil and gas companies have signed deals with thousands of landowners just like the Carters. The drillers hire hundreds of workers, lease property from landowners, pay royalties to landowners, and pay taxes and fees to local governments. "You have whole communities essentially that have won the lottery because of the lease payments," said Tom Murphy of Penn State University in 2008.

SOMETHING IN THE WATER

But for those with drilling rigs on their land, as well as for their neighbors who haven't signed deals with drillers, the gas boom isn't all rosy. Many formerly placid rural communities have been turned into industrial zones, with heavy machinery, noise, fumes, and bright lights day and night. Each shale gas pad, or drilling area, covers 4 to 6 acres (1 to 2 hectares), which hold waste pits, chemical storage tanks, pipes, trucks, and other equipment.

Fracking involves mixing millions of gallons of water with sand and chemicals and then injecting it, under extremely high pressure, deep underground. The high-pressure mixture fractures the shale, allowing it to release the gas within the formation. Although drilling companies aren't required by law to disclose the exact mix of chemicals they use in fracking, the

Several hydraulic fracturing sites and the roads built to connect and service them are visible in this aerial view of a mountaintop on the Roan Plateau in Colorado.

fluids are known to contain a wide variety of cancer-causing substances, including benzene, toluene, and xylene. Underground, the drilling fluid stirs up more harmful substances, such as heavy metals, brine, and radioactive minerals. All these substances come spewing up to the surface with the fracking water used during gas extraction.

In some states, such as Pennsylvania, most wastewater from fracking is stored onsite and then cleaned at sewage treatment plants. In other states, including Arkansas, Oklahoma, Colorado, Ohio, and Texas, the wastewater is injected thousands of feet underground into cement-lined pits. But toxic wastewater often leaks from storage tanks and underground pits into aquifers (natural underground reserves of freshwater), drinking water wells, rivers, and lakes.

The neighbors along Carter Road, who draw their water

from underground wells, began to see worrisome signs in 2008. One woman pulled clothes from her washing machine and found that they were dirtier than when they had gone in. One family found black, greasy sediment in their well. Another neighbor said that he could light his well water on fire with a match. A couple who owned horses said that the animals had vomited after drinking water from their well. With undrinkable well water, the Carter Road families had to buy bottled water for cooking, drinking, and washing.

> Where fracking water has been injected deep underground, geologists have recorded an increase in earthquake activity—in places that don't normally experience quakes.

Similar stories of foul-smelling, foamy brown well water have surfaced across Pennsylvania, Ohio, West Virginia, and other gas-drilling states. Sometimes methane, a major component of natural gas, has seeped into water wells, pipes, and homes and caused explosions, including one on Carter Road. And where fracking water has been injected deep underground, geologists have recorded an increase in earthquake activity—in places that don't normally experience quakes. Scientists explain that deep wastewater deposits cause small earthquakes by putting stress on existing fault lines. Although usually minor, the quakes have caused damage to some roads and buildings.

On top of this, fracking is a tremendous drain on freshwater supplies. Over its lifetime, each shale gas well requires between 2.4 and 7.8 million gallons (9 to 30 million liters) of freshwater, which drillers pump from lakes, streams, and aquifers. But across the United States (and around the world), freshwater supplies are dwindling due to drought, pollution, and overuse. Diverting millions of gallons for fracking only exacerbates the shortage. Yet because the demand for gas—and the profits it generates—is so great, the practice continues.

HOLDING THE LINE

In 2009 members of fifteen Carter Road households filed a lawsuit against Cabot Oil & Gas. They sought financial compensation from Cabot for contamination of their water, loss of their property values, and damage to their property. "I've gone to every congressman, representative . . . DEP [the state department of environmental protection], Cabot, anyone I could think of to bring this issue to the forefront," said a Carter Road resident when the lawsuit began. "We couldn't get help anywhere. . . . We're not greedy people. We just want some justice for something terribly wrong that happened here."

Around the nation, other landowners have filed lawsuits against frackers. Lawmakers and activists have called for tighter regulations of drilling operations, more inspectors, and higher penalties for gas companies that violate environmental safety rules. Vermont banned fracking altogether in 2012. New York banned the practice in 2014, and North Carolina implemented temporary bans while the state studies the impacts of fracking on the environment. A movement is also under way to restrict or prohibit fracking in California, where the technique is used to release oil as well as gas from shale formations. The state has been in a severe drought since the first decade of the twenty-first century. Opponents point out that fracking, with its massive water requirements, will further reduce dwindling supplies of water that's desperately needed for drinking and agriculture in California.

But fracking and natural gas development have many proponents as well. Many labor unions and local workers embrace the stable jobs that recent development projects have created. "The shale became a lifesaver and a lifeline for a lot of working families," notes Dennis Martire of the Laborers' International Union, which represents construction workers.

More broadly, energy companies and many politicians argue that the shale gas boom guarantees decades of energy

FRACKING IN CHINA

In China, where fracking operations began in the second decade of the twenty-first century, shale gas is located two or three times deeper underground than it is in the United States. Accessing the deep gas deposits is a dangerous, dirty, and expensive operation. In the mountain village of Jiaoshizhen, residents reported a massive explosion at a gas drilling operation in April 2013. Eight workers were killed. Fracking operations have also polluted streams and agricultural fields in the village.

As in the United States, Jiaoshizhen residents are of two minds about gas development. On the one hand, they complain about fouled water, noise, and bad smells. On the other hand, the gas company pays farmers about $1,475 per acre (0.4 hectares) per year to drill on their land. That is significantly more than farmers can earn by growing crops and is a difficult offer to refuse.

self-sufficiency for the United States. President Obama praised natural gas extraction in his 2012 State of the Union address, pointing out that in US shale formations, "we have a supply of natural gas that can last America nearly 100 years."

In addition, energy companies say that fracking can be made safer, with less wastewater to potentially contaminate wells and waterways. New practices include reusing fracking fluids rather than using clean water to frack wells; better treatment methods to remove salt and chemicals from used fracking water, making it suitable for watering crops and even drinking; and using gaseous gels and foams instead of water to frack shale. Technology companies are working on all these options.

Despite controversy over fracking, shale gas development is growing. In 2009 Exxon and Royal Dutch Shell purchased small shale gas companies, thereby bringing Big Oil into the shale gas business. Thousands of new gas wells continue to be drilled across the United States and around the world.

NORTH DAKOTA GOES BOOM

When people think of oil drilling, they usually think of shafts being sunk deep into the ground, straight down, to reach an oil deposit. That's how it's been done for many years. But new drills can also send horizontal branches off the main vertical shaft to pump oil sandwiched between horizontal layers of rock. Horizontal drilling technology has been a driving force in North America's new oil boom, especially in the US state of North Dakota.

The Bakken Shale formation stretches beneath northwestern North Dakota into northeastern Montana and up into Saskatchewan in Canada. The US Geological Survey estimates that the formation holds three to four billion barrels of "tight oil"—crude oil that is trapped between layers of shale—about 2 miles (3.2 km) underground. Geologists have known about the Bakken formation since 1953, but for much of the late twentieth century, drilling technology wasn't sophisticated enough to extract tight oil. With the development of horizontal drilling in the 1990s and fracking during the first decade of the twenty-first century, oil companies were at last able to access the Bakken oil.

By 2014 North Dakota was producing nine hundred thousand barrels of oil per day. The state's economy has flourished. Jobs are plentiful and well paying, and as a result, the state has the lowest unemployment rate in the nation. North Dakota oil workers—even those with only a high school degree—earn an average of $90,000 a year. Residents have money to spend, and banks, stores, restaurants, hotels, and other businesses are benefiting from the economic explosion. Formerly sleepy small towns with dwindling populations have been revived and energized. On a larger scale, North Dakota's shale oil production has significantly boosted the US oil supply and allowed the United States to begin exporting some of its oil, which has helped drive down the global price of petroleum.

Even so, shale oil development concerns many residents. Oil

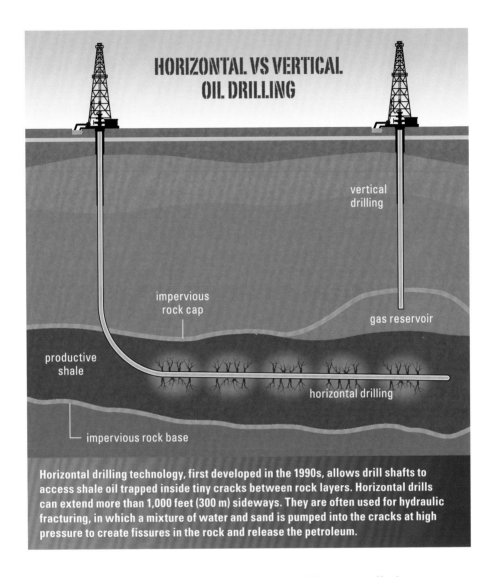

HORIZONTAL VS VERTICAL OIL DRILLING

vertical drilling

impervious rock cap

gas reservoir

productive shale

horizontal drilling

impervious rock base

Horizontal drilling technology, first developed in the 1990s, allows drill shafts to access shale oil trapped inside tiny cracks between rock layers. Horizontal drills can extend more than 1,000 feet (300 m) sideways. They are often used for hydraulic fracturing, in which a mixture of water and sand is pumped into the cracks at high pressure to create fissures in the rock and release the petroleum.

wells in North Dakota are set up much like gas wells in Pennsylvania: drillers build well pads near homes and farms and pay landowners for the rights to drill there. But in North Dakota and many other western states, most residents own only the surface rights to their land—that is, the right to farm, raise animals, or build structures there. In most places, the mineral rights—ownership of anything that sits below the surface, including oil and gas—were long ago sold to oil and gas companies. If an energy company wants to drill for oil in North Dakota and it has already purchased the mineral rights to a parcel of land, the homeowner or farmer has no say in the matter. The company must pay only a small fee to compensate residents for use of their land. Thus many North Dakotans have been forced to allow loud, dirty, and foul-smelling oil-drilling operations on their property.

AMERICAN INDIAN MINERAL RIGHTS

Some North Dakota residents, including American Indians living on reservations, still retain the full mineral rights to their land. But even these rights are not always secure. For instance, residents of the Fort Berthold Indian Reservation in west-central North Dakota lost their mineral rights in what many say was a swindle. A few tribal members and outside businesses bought up the mineral rights to thousands of acres of tribal land at low prices and then resold them to drillers for vast profits. Leaders of the three tribes (the Mandan, the Hidatsa, and the Arikara, also called the Three Affiliated Tribes) that occupy the reservation say their members were cheated out of billions of dollars that they would have gotten had the rights been originally sold for fair-market prices, with standard industry leases.

The US Department of the Interior is responsible for overseeing the development of oil and gas resources on tribal lands and for ensuring that development decisions are made in the best interest of tribal members. Critics charge that by allowing the sale and resale of the mineral rights at Fort Berthold, the Department of the Interior was negligent in protecting tribal members' interests. A group of tribal landowners filed a lawsuit against the individuals and businesses involved in the original purchases, charging them with financial misdeeds. But an attorney for one of the purchasers says that the group did nothing wrong. "This is a case of seller's remorse," he wrote, claiming that his client and his partners, "like anyone else in America, were perfectly entitled to try to obtain leases . . . on the best possible economic terms." For other North Dakota residents who hope to hold onto their mineral rights, the case of Fort Berthold presents a worrisome example.

Some North Dakota residents, including American Indians living on reservations, still retain the full mineral rights to their land. But even these rights are not always secure.

"People feel powerless," says Derrick Braaten, a Bismarck, North Dakota, attorney who represents landowners trying to fight oil companies. "The oil company is coming on your property. You don't have the ability to protect the land. You can push the monster back, but at a certain point it's gonna walk on top of you."

Once oil companies have the legal right to drill for shale oil, locals have even more causes for complaint. Since 2006, when the oil boom began in North Dakota, thousands of acres of rural farmland—previously home to fields of wheat, alfalfa, oat, flax, and corn—have turned into industrial zones, with multi-acre well pads, waste storage tanks, newly built roads, dust, air pollution, water pollution, oil and gas fumes, and litter. Streams and wells have been poisoned, and animals and people have become sick from exposure to toxic chemicals. To escape the industrial pollution, thousands of North Dakotans have put their homes up for sale, but many can't find buyers.

Further pollution is tied to the drilling process itself. In the Bakken Shale, as in other oil-drilling areas, billions of cubic feet of natural gas come to the surface along with oil pumped from underground. But the remote rural areas in which drilling is taking place don't have the pipeline infrastructure to capture the gas for heating and other uses. Instead, drillers simply burn off the gas at flaring stations near wells, a practice that is not prohibited by North Dakota laws or regulations. Every day, drillers in North Dakota burn 100 million cubic feet (2.8 million cu. m) of natural gas, enough to power a city of five hundred thousand people. This flaring releases about 6 million tons (5.4 million metric tons) of carbon dioxide into the atmosphere each year. Some companies have begun to build pipelines and facilities for processing the gas for fuel—including fuel for drilling operations. State lawmakers and regulators have called for new limits on gas flaring, but these efforts are minor compared to the amount of gas that is being flared. Experts don't expect a significant decrease in gas flaring in North Dakota until the 2020s.

Flaring isn't the only environmentally hazardous practice associated with shale oil extraction. Like other oil and gas operations, drilling operations in North Dakota involve vast amounts of freshwater, produced water, fracking fluids, and other fluids. Drillers have filled the Bakken landscape with plastic-lined pits to hold these liquids. However, an investigation by the news organization ProPublica discovered more

Natural gas is flared near an electric pumping unit at a crude oil well site outside of South Heart, North Dakota.

than one thousand accidental leaks of oil, fracking wastewater, and drilling fluids in North Dakota in 2011 alone. "In rainy springs like we had in 2011 and 2012 the pits overflow," says Derrick Braaten. "Plastic pit liners wear out and tear. The life of chemicals [in the wastewater] is much longer than the life of liners. Those wastes are going to move over time."

Despite pushes for improved regulations, opponents of shale oil drilling are not optimistic about the state's environmental future. In 2013 one oil worker made a grim assessment: "I'm 62 years old and I've worked 40 years in oil fields all over the country, but I've never seen any place like this. It's a free-for-all out here. It will be a toxic waste dump. No one will be able to live here."

"We can't impede on the right of the mineral owners to develop their minerals," explained Allison Ritter of the North Dakota Industrial Commission, a state agency. "[The protection of mineral rights is] in our state constitution."

North Dakota governor Jack Dalrymple disagrees. "[The oil rush] certainly isn't pleasant for everybody, but I think most people realize that once they kind of get over this period of furious drilling activity, it's really going to be a great thing for that part of the state."

In any case, state government supports continued shale oil development. "We can't impede on the right of the mineral owners to develop their minerals," explained Allison Ritter of the North Dakota Industrial Commission, a state agency. "[The protection of mineral rights is] in our state constitution." In fact, the commission announced in 2013 that over the next fifteen years, oil companies would drill an additional thirty-five thousand wells in North Dakota, increasing production to 2 million barrels per day.

TAR WARS

The United States is not the only North American country pursuing a petroleum revolution. The oil reserves in neighboring Canada are the third largest in the world, surpassed only by Saudi Arabia's and Venezuela's. Most of that oil is in the northern part of the province of Alberta and exists in the form of tar sands—thick, heavy bitumen mixed with sand and clay. For many years, oil companies mined only small amounts of Alberta tar sands, because the bitumen was difficult to separate from the surrounding soil. Traditional mining methods involve digging up the soil and then separating the bitumen from surrounding minerals, a labor-intensive and time-consuming process. But in the late 1990s, engineers devised a much simpler and faster technology for mining tar sands. They began to inject superhot steam deep underground to heat and liquefy bitumen, allowing it to be pumped to the surface. This method, known as steam extraction, yielded large amounts of bitumen, and companies began to invest heavily in Canadian tar sands operations.

Since the early twenty-first century, tar sands drilling operations have boomed, relying on both steam extraction and traditional mining techniques. Oil has brought thousands of jobs and billions of dollars to Alberta.

However, tar sands development has also brought industrialization and related environmental destruction. Roads and pipelines crisscross what was once a pristine northern Alberta wilderness that was habitat for bear, moose, caribou, and migrating birds and also home to many First Nations peoples (indigenous Canadians).

The drilling itself is even more environmentally damaging than the infrastructure. Both traditional mining and steam

This aerial view was taken in 2008 near Fort McMurray, a town in Alberta, Canada. It shows miles of roads constructed as part of the development for mining tar sands in a formerly pristine wilderness.

extraction require large amounts of water—up to three barrels of water for every barrel of extracted oil. Tar sands bitumen is more poisonous than ordinary crude oil. It contains more lead, sulfur, benzene, and other toxins, and these substances end up in wastewater from tar sands operations. By 2013 tar sands mining in Alberta was producing 400 million gallons (1,500 million liters) of contaminated water per day. Companies store the wastewater in giant artificial ponds, but some ponds have leaked, and toxic water has run into lakes and rivers, killing fish and other wildlife. In addition, migrating birds often mistake the poisonous ponds for natural lakes. They land on the ponds and drink the deadly water.

KEYSTONE XL

Tar sands oil from Alberta is shipped to refineries in the United States and Canada on trains and trucks and through pipelines. To move even more oil to refineries, the TransCanada Corporation proposed an expansion of the Keystone Pipeline, which runs from Alberta to the southern United States.

Much of the Keystone expansion (or Keystone XL) has been in operation since early 2014—with the exception of its northern portion, the fourth and final stage of construction. Environmentalists oppose this branch of the expansion, fearing the new pipeline could burst or leak and contaminate farmland and underwater drinking supplies. "We know these pipelines leak," said John Harter, who fought to keep the Keystone XL from crossing his farm in South Dakota, ". . . and they [oil companies] know they're going to leak."

TransCanada has insisted that fears of a spill are wildly exaggerated. From company headquarters in Calgary, Alberta, computers monitor the flow of oil through the existing pipeline second by second, and engineers can quickly shut down sections of the pipeline in the event of a leak. Nebraska hydrogeologist James Goeke noted, "A spill wouldn't be nice, but it would certainly be restricted to within a half-mile [0.8 km] of the pipeline."

Because Keystone XL's controversial northern section would cross the Canadian–US border, it cannot be built without permission of the US president. This has put Barack Obama at the center of the Keystone XL debate. He delayed making a decision, expressing concerns about the ecosystems in the pipeline's path, such as the vast Ogallala Aquifer, which supplies drinking water to millions of farms and homes. In November 2014, impatient with the president's delays, Congressional lawmakers proposed a bill to greenlight the extension. The bill was defeated in the Senate but was followed by another bill in January 2015. This second bill passed both houses of Congress, but the Obama administration indicated that the president would veto the bill. With both sides ready for a fight, the controversy seemed far from over.

Yet, according to some experts, the Keystone XL question is losing its urgency. In October 2014, TransCanada announced plans to build another pipeline along a different route—one that will not cross the border and thus will not require approval of the US president. This exclusively Canadian pipeline will transport oil eastward instead of southward, bypassing the ecologically fragile areas through which the northern Keystone XL branch would have passed. As a result, many analysts predict that the Keystone expansion will be shelved indefinitely, with both the oil industry and its opponents focusing on other projects. As energy expert Michael Levi notes, "It's always been clear that . . . slowing Keystone wasn't going to stop the flow of Canadian oil."

President Barack Obama visits the TransCanada Stillwater Pipe Yard in Cushing, Oklahoma in 2012. TransCanada has pushed President Obama to approve the final phase of its expansion of the Keystone pipeline, which would carry crude oil from Canada's tar sands through several US states to Gulf port cities.

Additional pollutants come out of the refining process. After extraction, tar sands bitumen undergoes a process called coking to separate liquid oil from solid bitumen. Coking creates a by-product called petroleum coke, which is high in sulfur and carbon, both known pollutants. Tar sands operators store this coke in piles and pits around mining sites in Alberta. Some of it is shipped overseas to China, Mexico, India, and elsewhere. There, the carbon- and sulfur-heavy coke is burned for fuel, and the resulting smokestack emissions exacerbate air pollution in already heavily polluted cities. Back in Alberta, winds sometimes carry coke particles from unenclosed piles out over surrounding communities. Local citizens worry that this dust threatens their health.

CARBON BOMB

Even after refining, tar sands oil contains more carbon dioxide than ordinary crude oil, and it therefore releases more carbon into the atmosphere when burned. This is why climate scientists refer to tar sands oil as a carbon bomb. They believe that burning tar sands oil from Alberta and other regions (including eastern Utah in the United States, Venezuela, and the Middle East) will push global climate change past the point of no return.

Scientists say that once the amount of carbon dioxide in the atmosphere reaches 450 parts per million (450 molecules of carbon dioxide for each million of other molecules in the atmosphere), climate change will begin to accelerate—and nothing will be able to slow or stop it, even if humans stop burning fossil fuels. That's because over the next few decades, melting ice at the North and South Poles will release billions of tons of methane, a greenhouse gas. The gas will increase warming further and melt more polar ice—creating an ongoing cycle.

With this in mind, scientist James Hansen, then with NASA,

> Scientists say that once the amount of carbon dioxide in the atmosphere reaches 450 parts per million, climate change will begin to accelerate—and nothing will be able to slow or stop it, even if humans stop burning fossil fuels.

wrote in 2011 that adding the Alberta tar sands to existing fossil fuels would be "game over for the climate." He predicted, in the coming decades, long-term droughts, heavy flooding, and the devastation of agricultural areas. In the long run, he foresees disintegration of the polar ice sheets, coastal cities flooded by rising seas, and intolerable global temperatures.

But others contend that ending tar sands development would be impractical. Ed Stelmach, former premier of the province of Alberta, stresses, "We can all agree that alternative energy sources are part of the supply equation to power our future. But until those alternatives are developed commercially—and at a price that consumers can afford—we still require the oil and gas to power our lives." Stelmach also explains that technological developments have lowered the carbon-intensity of oil from the tar sands and will continue to do so. "Between 1990 and 2008," he remarks, "the oil sands industry reduced average per barrel greenhouse gas emissions from production by 39 percent."

POLAR PETROLEUM

The last frontier for petroleum development lies at the top of the world. According to a 2008 study by the US Geological Survey, the Arctic Ocean and surrounding lands hold 90 billion barrels of oil and 1.7 trillion cubic feet (0.5 trillion cubic meters) of natural gas. Experts estimate that the Chukchi Sea north of Alaska, for example, has underwater oil fields to rival any found in Texas or Saudi Arabia.

> "It is an irony as biting as the frigid temperatures that will [come in the Arctic] in the autumn that the very oil companies that contributed so much to global warming now stand to benefit from the dramatic melt it is causing."
>
> –Charles M. Sennott, journalist

Previously, drilling for oil and gas in the Arctic was extremely difficult. Most of the year, ice choked Arctic waterways, so ships couldn't travel freely to bring workers, drilling platforms, and other equipment to drilling sites. Due to climate change, however, ice at the North and South Poles is melting. According to NASA, each year the Arctic Ocean loses about 30,000 square miles (78,000 sq. km) of sea ice—an area about the size of the state of Maine. As polar ice melts, newly open waters provide increased access to oil fields.

After securing oil leases in Arctic areas owned by the United States, Royal Dutch Shell began offshore drilling in the Chukchi Sea in 2012. The project was beset by problems, including equipment failures and weather delays, and was put on hold. But Shell hopes to return to the sea in the summer of 2015. A consortium of companies including BP, Exxon, Mobil, and Imperial Oil has submitted an application to Canada to drill in the Beaufort Sea. In addition, Russia, Sweden, Greenland, Iceland, Norway, and Finland are all gearing up to allow companies to drill in Arctic areas under their control.

Environmentalists fear that oil drilling will devastate Arctic regions, which are home to caribou, polar bears, whales, and other wildlife, as well as to indigenous peoples. Opponents would like to halt Arctic oil drilling completely or at the very least impose tighter safety restrictions, such as requiring the use of double-walled pipelines and equipment designed to withstand the force of moving ice. In 2013 the US Department of the

Interior noted serious doubts about whether Shell specifically could "operate safely and responsibly in the challenging and unpredictable conditions" of the Arctic.

But the scramble to extract Arctic oil and gas continues, and this extraction will cause further climate change and more melting of polar ice. Writes journalist Charles M. Sennott, "It is an irony as biting as the frigid temperatures that will [come in the Arctic] in the autumn that the very oil companies that contributed so much to global warming now stand to benefit from the dramatic melt it is causing."

CHAPTER SIX

FUELING THE FUTURE

It takes hundreds of millions of years for the forces of nature—heat, pressure, decomposition, and various chemical reactions—to create petroleum out of the remains of plants and animals. Douglas C. Elliott can do basically the same thing in less than an hour. Elliott, lead investigator at the US Department of Energy's Pacific Northwest National Laboratory in Richland, Washington, has fine-tuned a process called hydrothermal liquefaction. The system uses high heat and high pressure to turn a mixture of algae and water into oil that is chemically similar to crude oil. The algae oil can be easily refined into jet fuel, diesel fuel, or gasoline. If Elliott's technique can be developed on a wide scale, algae oil could be sold for as little as two dollars a gallon.

Unlike carbon-based fossil fuels, the oil from algae is an example of a renewable fuel—a resource that can be replenished as needed. Renewable fuels are appealing for two reasons. First, as Earth's fossil fuels are depleted, alternative sources of energy will become essential. Second, renewable fuels are generally less harmful to human, plant, and animal life than fossil fuels.

Consider algae oil. It is very low in toxins. When burned, it does release carbon, which contributes to climate change, but the carbon emissions from burning algae oil are 50 to 70 percent less than those released by the burning of petroleum. And unlike petroleum, which has to be transported thousands of miles via ships, trucks, trains, and pipelines—with the risk of spills along the way—algae oil could be produced in natural or artificial ponds and used nearby, reducing or potentially eliminating the necessity of long-distance transportation.

A FORK IN THE ROAD

Sun power, wind power, hydropower, and geothermal power are other examples of renewable energy that are in use and under development in various parts of the world. But it's easy to doubt that renewable energy could supply enough fuel to run our cars, heat our homes, and power our machines. After all, in 2012 renewable fuels accounted for just 19 percent of global energy use. Is it possible to reach 100 percent or even 50 percent? Some people say yes, provided the necessary infrastructure is put in place. In a 2009 *Scientific American* article, a team of researchers from Stanford University in California wrote, "Our plan calls for millions of wind turbines, water machines [hydroelectric facilities] and solar installations. The numbers are large . . . but society has achieved massive transformations before."

Transformation has already begun in automobile and fuel technologies. Cars sold in the United States are more fuel efficient than cars of the past. During his first term in office, President Obama raised fuel-efficiency standards, requiring cars and light trucks sold in the United States to achieve an average fuel efficiency of 35.5 miles (57 km) per gallon of gas. During his second term, Obama raised fuel-efficiency standards again, calling for an average of 54.5 miles (88 km) per gallon by 2025. To achieve this goal, automakers will have to redesign engines, use lighter materials (it takes less fuel to move a lighter car), and design more aerodynamic cars. Renewable energy also has a role to play.

A plant-based liquid called ethanol, usually made from corn or sugarcane, can be used to fuel cars. Nations around the world use tax breaks and legislation to encourage the use of ethanol fuel. Many kinds of ethanol are low in harmful toxins and, when burned, release less carbon than gasoline does. In the United States, most gasoline contains between 5 and 10 percent

HIGH ENERGY

In the United States, the Department of Energy (DOE) develops and coordinates national energy policies and programs. The department operates a network of laboratories and other facilities that research and design new, cleaner, and more efficient energy technologies and systems. The DOE also runs loan programs that help businesses pay for innovative energy-related projects.

Some DOE-sponsored projects involve innovations with solar, wind, and other renewable energy sources. Other projects focus on alternative-fuel vehicles, such as electric cars or those that run on biodiesel. The department also works with the traditional fossil fuels of coal, crude oil, and natural gas. For example, the department's Oil and Natural Gas program monitors the US petroleum industry and aims to "provide unbiased scientific information as a basis for regulation" through its research into safety issues and environmental concerns.

In addition, the DOE works to reduce greenhouse gas emissions and encourage energy savings. For instance, the department offers loans to automobile manufacturers to fund technologies that improve the fuel efficiency of gas-powered vehicles.

ethanol, a blend that works in ordinary passenger cars. But some new cars can burn fuel made of 85 and even 100 percent ethanol. Cars that run on 100 percent ethanol are common in Brazil, for example.

In the first decade of the twenty-first century, several Americans made headlines by driving cross-country in cars that burned only used cooking grease. The cars had diesel engines that had been converted to accommodate the grease. The drivers stopped at fast-food restaurants and siphoned grease from waste tanks for free. Most restaurant managers were happy to cooperate, since they normally pay to have someone haul the grease away. These trips were evidence of a keen interest in biodiesel (diesel fuel made from grease, soybeans, algae, animal fats, and other biological substances). The biodiesel industry is growing. Many buses and trucks run on biodiesel. Some vehicles run on a blend of biodiesel and ordinary diesel fuel. Biodiesel is far less polluting and releases far less carbon than petroleum-based fuels when burned.

A research associate at Sapphire Energy, Inc., in San Diego, California, handles containers of water containing algae. The algae is cultivated for biofuel—a crude oil that can be processed in existing refineries to create jet fuel, diesel fuel, and gasoline. Scientists are seeking to find alternatives like this to standard, petroleum-based sources of power.

The most fuel-efficient cars so far are those that run partly or entirely on electricity. The Toyota Prius is the most well-known example of a hybrid electric car—a vehicle that contains both a gasoline engine and an electric battery. Hybrid cars combine the best features of gasoline-powered cars (the ability to run at least 300 miles [483 km] between fuel stops along with easy and quick refueling), with the best features of electric cars (no emissions to pollute the air or contribute to climate change and no need to buy expensive gas). In the Prius and other hybrid cars, some of the energy from the gasoline-powered engine goes to recharge the car's battery during use. Drivers can also buy plug-in hybrids, which plug into specialized electrical outlets for recharging. These cars rely more on electricity and less on gasoline than do conventional hybrid cars.

All-electric cars also need recharging, which drivers can do at home or at commercial recharging stations. Charging an all-electric car usually takes between three and eight hours, depending on the model, and vehicles can travel between 60 and 120 miles (97 to 193 km) on a full charge. The long charging time and the limited mileage can be a real drawback for drivers. But owners of all-electric cars see a big savings in fueling costs. A gallon of gasoline can cost up to four dollars and will get the typical car about 30 miles (48 km) down the road. In an electric car, that same 30 miles will cost the driver just sixty cents.

From an environmental standpoint, electric cars have pluses and minuses. Electric cars don't release harmful pollution or greenhouse gases, but most electricity comes from burning coal or natural gas, and coal burning especially creates vast amounts of pollution and carbon emissions. Nuclear power is also used to generate electricity. Although nuclear power plants do not release solid or gas pollutants into the atmosphere, they do produce deadly radioactive waste, and if they malfunction, they can release hazardous radiation. The cleanest option for charging an electric car (or any electric device) is to use electricity generated with solar power—and around the world, more and more solar charging stations are coming online.

Another breakthrough in alternative-fuel technology has emerged in the form of hydrogen-powered cars. This kind of car contains devices called fuel cells, which mix hydrogen gas and oxygen to generate electricity that powers the car. The only emissions from a hydrogen car are water vapor, warm air, and hydrogen. Yet these pollution-free results come at the cost of a complex fuel production process. The necessary oxygen used by the fuel cells can be drawn from the air around the car, but the hydrogen is more challenging to obtain. Though hydrogen is the most abundant element in the universe, it doesn't exist on its own. It is an ingredient in chemical compounds, such as hydrocarbons. To get hydrogen for fuel cells, scientists process natural gas, separating the hydrogen from the carbon. Most methods of hydrogen production emit carbon dioxide, although far less than the burning of fossil fuels produces. But scientists say that green technology such as solar or wind power can be used to create a cleaner production process. And natural gas isn't the only source of useable hydrogen. The element can also be separated from water, sewage, or animal waste.

Leading automobile companies have begun manufacturing hydrogen cars. Toyota will introduce the first mass-market hydrogen car, the Mirai, in 2015. It will cost about $57,000, far more than most gasoline-powered or electric car, but experts expect the price to drop sharply as hydrogen fuel cell technology improves. Worldwide, car companies and other energy organizations are installing public hydrogen fueling stations, where hydrogen gas can be pumped into the tanks of hydrogen cars.

> Most methods of hydrogen production emit carbon dioxide, although far less than the burning of fossil fuels produces.

IT'S A NATURAL

From an environmental standpoint, natural gas has advantages over crude oil and coal. When burned, natural gas releases 30 percent fewer carbon emissions than oil does and 60 percent fewer carbon emissions than coal. Therefore, it contributes less to climate change. Natural gas also produces less air pollution than other fossil fuels.

In the past, natural gas has been used primarily to heat homes and businesses. For generating electricity, people have traditionally burned coal. That's changing. In the twenty-first century, more and more electrical power plants are burning natural gas. In addition, engineers have designed natural-gas-powered vehicles, and their numbers are increasing on US roadways. In his 2014 State of the Union address, President Obama praised natural gas. He declared, "If extracted safely, [natural gas is] the bridge fuel that can power our economy with less of the carbon pollution that causes climate change."

So far, the United States has only thirteen hydrogen fueling stations, but that number is likely to rise. By the mid-2020s, the state of California is expected to have one hundred hydrogen fueling stations.

MORE OR LESS?

In the United States, most of the petroleum Americans use (about 70 percent) goes to transportation fuel, so switching to electric and biofuel vehicles would go a long way toward reducing petroleum use. But what about the other 30 percent—the oil used for heating and for fertilizer, lubricants, detergents, paints, and plastics? Alternatives do exist. Solar and other renewable fuels can be used for heating, and some companies sell products that don't contain petrochemicals at all. For example, scientists have developed bioplastics, made from the starch found in corn, wheat, potatoes, and other vegetables. After disposal, these plastics break down into harmless substances, with no ill environmental effects. These products and renewable sources of energy tend to be much more expensive than similar products made from petrochemicals, however, and are not widely used.

Earth-friendly options, however promising, are likely to make only a small dent in overall petroleum use. That's because, globally, more cars are on the roads than ever before. Particularly in China and India, the economy is growing and more people are able to afford cars. In fact, since 2009, car sales in China have surpassed those in the United States. And even if electric and solar-powered cars became widely used, the tires, foam, resin, and plastics found in and on those cars would likely still be made with petroleum. And the cars and components would most likely still be made in factories that run on fossil fuels. As for alternative fuels, they all have drawbacks and limitations. For instance,

These utensils were made using a biodegradable starch-polyester material. Unlike plastic utensils, these bioplastics will break down over time, causing no harm to the environment.

A traffic jam stalls vehicles in downtown Bangkok, Thailand. Worldwide, more cars than ever before are increasing the demand for petroleum products, from the gasoline used as fuel to the plastics used for car parts.

algae oil and ethanol still release carbon dioxide into the air when burned. And to power even a fraction of US cars with ethanol, Americans have had to set aside large amounts of farmland to grow the corn to make the fuel. This has cut down on the availability of corn for food and other uses, which in turn has driven up global corn prices—effects that are felt most strongly in developing countries, where corn is a crucial food source for both humans and livestock. In a world where hunger on a massive scale is a reality, this use of farmland is controversial.

One factor that might prompt people to use less petroleum is cost. History shows that when the price of gasoline increases, people drive less. In Europe gasoline costs more than twice as much as it does in the United States. So Europeans drive more fuel-efficient cars, ride bicycles more often, and rely more on mass transit such as buses and trains. If prices rose high enough in the United States, many Americans might be motivated to make similar changes. But a large-scale transition would still present challenges, particularly in the public transportation sector. In the United States, subways or light-rail systems operate only in large and mid-sized cities, and bus service is spotty around the country. In many places, cars are the only option for crosstown travel, leaving people no choice but to drive. And rather than lobbying for more public transportation options, many families simply direct more of their monthly income to covering the cost of gas when prices rise.

Just 1.5 percent of Chevron's expenditures went toward alternative fuels in 2012—down from 2.8 percent in 2008.

BIG OIL, SMALL CHANGES

Of course, not everyone envisions a future where people use less petroleum. Oil companies have a vested interest in keeping vast amounts of petroleum flowing to consumers for the foreseeable future. In the 1980s, Big Oil made small investments in renewable energy, and oil companies have claimed to embrace the potential of alternative fuels. For instance, in 2000 BP ran a marketing campaign claiming that its initials stood for "Beyond Petroleum." In 2010 a Chevron ad announced, "It's time oil companies get behind the development of renewable energy." But critics accuse the companies of greenwashing—attempting to convince the public that they are committed to alternative fuels while the numbers tell a different story. Just 1.5 percent of Chevron's expenditures went toward alternative fuels in 2012—down from 2.8 percent in 2008. The rest went toward finding, extracting, and selling oil and gas. Other oil companies spend even less on renewable energy—and the amounts have decreased in recent years. BP got out of the solar energy business in 2011 and sold off its sixteen US wind farms in 2013. Chevron had pulled out of its investments in biofuels by 2013, and in 2014, it sold off an offshoot company called Chevron Energy Solutions, which focused on solar power and energy efficiency.

Why is Big Oil reluctant to invest in technologies that could boost public goodwill and offer new sources of revenue? One reason is that renewable energy simply doesn't promise the same levels of profit that companies know they can expect from oil and gas. Energy analyst Daniel Choi summed up Big Oil's dilemma: "I have this much money to spend. Am I going to use it to buy new plots of land, to develop this plot of land [for oil and gas production], or will I allot it to investing in a new renewable energy company?" In addition, newly accessible and large oil and gas supplies available in the United States, Canada, the Arctic, and elsewhere have prompted oil companies to refocus their investments on their core business: petroleum.

THE END OF OIL

Regardless of how the world approaches its energy needs, people will someday have to stop using petroleum—because eventually the planet's petroleum supply will be completely depleted. When will that happen? In 1956 US geologist Marion King Hubbert introduced a concept called peak oil. He predicted that oil production, which had been increasing since the 1850s, would continue to increase until around 2006. At that point, he said, global oil production would then begin to decline as oil supplies on Earth became depleted. By about 2200, Hubbert said, all the oil would be gone.

Hubbert's forecast was wrong on at least one count: oil production did not peak in 2006. That year came and went, and production continued to climb. When Hubbert made his prediction, he didn't know about oil supplies yet to be found under the oceans. He didn't know that new technologies would allow companies to extract tar sands oil in Canada and shale oil in North Dakota. He didn't know about fracking and Marcellus Shale. He didn't know that melting polar ice would open up large areas of the Arctic to oil and gas exploration.

At some point, though, regardless of humanity's technological innovations and Earth's changing landscape, petroleum will run out. No one knows exactly when, but many experts have continued to make estimates. In 2013 the British Institution of Mechanical Engineers predicted that considering the rapidly increasing global population, the oil supply will be gone in about forty years. It is possible that vast new oil deposits will be discovered, changing all the predictions. But if the British engineers are right, you will see oil run out in your lifetime. You will see the Age of Oil come to an end.

SOURCE NOTES

4   Jeannette Reyes, "First Look at the Mayflower Oil Spill Rupture Site," *katv.com*, April 18, 2013, http://www.katv.com/story/21904029/mayflower-oil-spill-a-first-look-at-the-rupture-site.

8   Donald J. Boudreaux, "In Praise of Petroleum," *TribLive.com*, March 13, 2012, http://triblive.com/x/pittsburghtrib/opinion/columnists/boudreaux/s_786137.html#axzz2pAumdkYD.

12 "President Bush's State of the Union Address," *Washington Post*, January 31, 2006, http://www.washingtonpost.com/wp-dyn/content/article/2006/01/31/AR2006013101468.html.

12 "Economic Impacts of the Oil and Natural Gas Industry on the US Economy in 2011," American Petroleum Institute, July 2013, accessed October 1, 2014, http://www.api.org/~/media/Files/Policy/Jobs/Economic_impacts_Ong_2011.pdf.

17 Emory Dean Keoke and Marie Kay Porterfield, *Encyclopedia of American Indian Contributions to the World: 15,000 Years of Inventions and Innovations* (New York: Facts on File, 2001), 22–23.

21 Daniel Yergin, *The Quest: Energy, Security, and the Remaking of the Modern World* (New York: Penguin Press, 2011), 230.

23 Daniel Yergin, *The Prize: The Epic Quest for Oil, Money and Power* (New York: Simon & Schuster, 1992), 343.

34 "Obama's Speech in Lansing, Michigan," *New York Times*, August 4, 2008, http://www.nytimes.com/2008/08/04/us/politics/04text-obama.html?pagewanted=all&_r=1&.

35 Clifford Krauss, "In North Dakota, Flames of Wasted Natural Gas Light the Prairie," *New York Times*, September 26, 2011, http://www.nytimes.com/2011/09/27/business/energy-environment/in-north-dakota-wasted-natural-gas-flickers-against-the-sky.html?pagewanted=all.

38 Daniel Gilbert and Justin Scheck, "Big Oil Companies Struggle to Justify Soaring Project Costs," *Wall Street Journal*, January 28, 2014, http://online.wsj.com/news/articles/SB10001424052702303277704579348332283819314.

40 Juhasz, *Tyranny of Oil*, 217.

41 Javier Sierra, "The Fox in Her Henhouse," Sierra Club, accessed August 1, 2014, http://www.sierraclub.org/ecocentro/ingles/column2006-03.asp.

42 Nate Hagens, "Complaining about Mosquito Bites While a Crocodile Bites Our Leg," Post Carbon Institute, May 2, 2011, available online at Resilience, http://www.resilience.org/stories/2011-05-02/complaining-about-mosquito-bites-while-crocodile-bites-our-leg.

44 Ben Rooney, "Big Oil's $38 Billion Defense," *CNN Money*, April 29, 2011, http://money.cnn.com/2011/04/29/news/companies/big-oil-gas-price -response.

44 Donald J. Boudreaux, "In Defense of Big Oil: The Truth about Those Huge, Hated Earnings Numbers," *New York Daily News*, May 11, 2011, http://www.nydailynews.com/opinion/defense-big-oil-truth-huge -hated-earnings-numbers-article-1.144253?comment=true.

44 Hagens, "Complaining about Mosquito Bites."

45 Juhasz, *Tyranny of Oil*, 273.

50 Zhuang Pinghui, "Water Supplies Return to Lanzhou after Benzene Spill, but Residents Are Wary," *South China Morning Post*, April 15, 2014, http://www.scmp.com/news/china/article/1482128/lanzhou-water -plant-replace-corroded-pipe-after-benzene-contamination.

55 Ian Urbina, "U.S. Said to Allow Drilling without Needed Permits," *New York Times*, May 13, 2010, http://www.nytimes.com/2010/05/14/ us/14agency.html?pagewanted=all.

55 "The Reorganization of the Former MMS," Bureau of Ocean Energy Management, accessed October 14, 2014, http://www.boem.gov/ Reorganization/.

55 Ibid.

55 Ibid.

56 Juhasz, *Tyranny of Oil*, 266.

56 Ibid.

59 Bob Dudley, "Annual General Meeting: Group Chief Executive," speech, BP, April 11, 2013, http://www.bp.com/en/global/corporate/press/ speeches/speech-by-bob-dudley-group-chief-executive-bp-at-bps -annual-general-meeting-11-april-2013.html.

61 Tom Wilber, *Under the Surface: Fracking, Fortunes, and the Fate of the Marcellus Shale* (Ithaca, NY: Cornell University Press, 2012), 44.

64 Ibid., 167.

64 Kevin Begos, Associated Press, "Fracking Draws Support from Unions as Jobs Flourish, Worrying Environmentalists," *Huffington Post*, April 20, 2014, http://www.huffingtonpost.com/2014/04/21/fracking-support _n_5182481.html.

65 F. William Engdahl, "The Fracked-Up USA Shale Gas Bubble," *Global Research*, March 13, 2013, http://www.globalresearch.ca/the-fracked-up -usa-shale-gas-bubble/5326504.

69 James William Gibson, "Bombing North Dakota," *Earth Island Journal*, Winter 2013, accessed May 26, 2014, http://www.earthisland.org/journal/index.php/eij/article/bombing_north_dakota.

68 Jack Nicas, "Shale-Oil Boom Divides Reservation," *Wall Street Journal*, February 28, 2013, http://online.wsj.com/news/articles/SB100014241278 87323293704578331030315441350.

71 Ibid.

71 Justin Mikulka, "'Wild West' Approach to Regulation in Bakken Shale Means Bomb Trains Continue to Roll," *Desmoblog.com*, October 7, 2014, http://www.desmogblog.com/2014/10/07/wild-west-approach -regulation-bakken-means-bomb-trains-continue-roll.

71 Ryan Holeywell, "North Dakota's Oil Boom Is a Blessing and a Curse," *Governing*, August 2011, accessed July 22, 2014, http://www.governing .com/topics/energy-env/north-dakotas-oil-boom-blessing-curse.html.

71 James William Gibson, "Bombing North Dakota," *Earth Island Journal*, Winter 2013, accessed May 26, 2014, http://www.earthisland.org/journal/index.php/eij/article/bombing_north_dakota.

71 Ibid.

74 Samuel Avery, *The Pipeline and the Paradigm: Keystone XL, Tar Sands, and the Battle to Defuse the Carbon Bomb* (Washington, DC: Ruka Press, 2013), 104.

74 Steven Mufson, "Keystone XL Pipeline May Threaten Aquifer that Irrigates Much of the Central U.S.," *Washington Post*, August 6, 2012, accessed November 24, 2014, http://www.washingtonpost.com/national/health-science/keystone-xl-pipeline-may-threaten-aquifer -that-irrigates-much-of-the-central-us/2012/08/06/7bf0215c-d4db-11e1 -a9e3-c5249ea531ca_story.html.

75 Angelo Young, "No Keystone XL Pipeline? No Problem, Says Canadian Firm Planning to Send Crude East Instead of South," *International Business Times*, October 8, 2014, http://www.ibtimes.com/no-keystone -xl-pipeline-no-problem-says-canadian-firm-planning-send-crude-east -instead-1701211.

76 Bill McKibben, *Oil and Honey: The Education of an Unlikely Activity* (New York: Times Books, 2013), 15.

77 Ed Stelmach, "In Defense of Oil Sands," *Politico*, July 16, 2010, http://dyn.politico.com/printstory.cfm?uuid=D982697C-18FE-70B2 -A8C5C985FC93D7D4.

77 Ibid.

78 Charles M. Sennott, "Arctic Melt Opens Door for Big Oil's Next Boom," *Global Post*, October 4, 2012, http://www.globalpost.com/dispatch/news/regions/americas/121003/arctic-melt-opens-door-big-oils-next-boom.

78 Chester Dawson, "Oil Giants Set Their Sights on Arctic Waters," *Wall Street Journal*, May 18, 2014, http://online.wsj.com/news/articles/SB100014240527023036784045795362404503320938.

79 Sennott, "Arctic Melt Opens Door for Big Oil's Next Boom."

81 Tara Lohan, "We Have the Energy We Need to Power the World—So What's Stopping Us?" Post Carbon Institute, November 11, 2013, http://www.resilience.org/stories/2013-11-11/we-have-the-renewable-energy-we-need-to-power-the-world-so-what-s-stopping-us.

82 "Shale Gas R&D," *Energy.gov*, accessed August 1, 2014, http://energy.gov/fe/science-innovation/oil-gas-research/shale-gas-rd.

86 Jeff Spross, "Why President Obama's Natural Gas 'Bridge' May Be on the Verge of Collapse," *Climate Progress*, January 30, 2014, http://thinkprogress.org/climate/2014/01/30/3224951/obama-sotu-natural-gas/#.

89 Antonia Juhasz, "Big Oil's Lies about Alternative Energy," *Rolling Stone*, June 25, 2013, http://www.rollingstone.com/politics/news/big-oils-big-lies-about-alternative-energy-20130625?print=true.

90 David Ferris and Nathaniel Gronewold, "Why the Oil Majors Are Backing Away from Renewable Energy," *E&E Publishing*, October 3, 2014, http://www.eenews.net/stories/1060006834.

GLOSSARY

fossil fuel: a fuel formed inside Earth from the remains of ancient plants or animals. Coal, crude oil, and natural gas are examples of fossil fuels.

greenhouse gas: a gas that trap heat in Earth's atmosphere. Examples include carbon dioxide and methane. Human activities such as the burning of fossil fuels have released extra greenhouse gases into the atmosphere, causing global climate change.

hydrocarbon: a substance containing only the elements hydrogen and carbon.

lease: a contract by which someone rents land, equipment, or a structure for a specific purpose, a specific length of time, and a specific amount of money.

molecule: the smallest particle of a substance that retains all the properties of the substance and is composed of one or more atoms.

oil: a thick, black mixture of hydrocarbons that comes from the ground. The term sometimes refers specifically to crude oil and sometimes includes both crude oil and bitumen.

petroleum: a mixture of hydrocarbons that can take the form of a solid (bitumen), liquid (crude oil), or gas (natural gas).

royalty: a share of the product or profits from an enterprise, given to someone who leases property to a company for commercial purposes

spermaceti: a waxy substance found in the heads of sperm whales and once highly valued as a clean-burning lamp fuel.

subcontractor: an individual or business hired to perform a portion of a large job for the business that signed the original contract.

SELECTED BIBLIOGRAPHY

Austen, Ian. "A Black Mountain of Canadian Oil Waste Is Rising over Detroit." *New York Times*, May 17, 2013. http://www.nytimes.com/2013/05/18/business/energy-environment/mountain-of-petroleum-coke-from-oil-sands-rises-in-detroit.html.

Avery, Samuel. *The Pipeline and the Paradigm: Keystone XL, Tar Sands, and the Battle to Defuse the Carbon Bomb*. Washington, DC: Ruka Press, 2013.

Bilkadi, Zayn. "Bitumen: A History." *Saudi Aramco World*, November/December 1984. https://www.saudiaramcoworld.com/issue/198406/bitumen.-.a.history.htm.

Black, Brian. *Crude Reality: Petroleum in World History*. Lanham, MD: Rowman & Littlefield, 2012.

Boudreaux, Donald J. "In Defense of Big Oil: The Truth about Those Huge, Hated Earnings Numbers." *New York Daily News*, May 11, 2011. http://www.nydailynews.com/opinion/defense-big-oil-truth-huge-hated-earnings-numbers-article-1.144253?comment=true.

Broder, John M. "Obama to Open Offshore Areas to Oil Drilling for First Time." *New York Times*, March 31, 2010. http://www.nytimes.com/2010/03/31/science/earth/31energy.html.

Caplan-Bricker, Nora. "This Is What Happens When a Pipeline Bursts in Your Town." *New Republic*, November 18, 2013. http://www.newrepublic.com/article/115624/exxon-oil-spill-arkansas-2013-how-pipeline-burst-mayflower.

Dawson, Chester. "Oil Giants Set Their Sights on Arctic Waters." *Wall Street Journal*, May 18, 2014. http://online.wsj.com/news/articles/SB10001424052702303678404579536240450320938.

Engdahl, F. William. "The Fracked-Up USA Shale Gas Bubble." *GlobalResearch*, March 13, 2013. http://www.globalresearch.ca/the-fracked-up-usa-shale-gas-bubble/5326504.

Gibson, James William. "Bombing North Dakota: Living amid the Bakken Oil Boom." *Earth Island Journal*, Winter 2013. Accessed May 26, 2014. http://www.earthisland.org/journal/index.php/eij/article/bombing_north_dakota.

Gilbert, Daniel, and Justin Scheck. "Big Oil Companies Struggle to Justify Soaring Project Costs." *Wall Street Journal*, January 28, 2014. http://online.wsj.com/news/articles/SB10001424052702303277704579348332283819314.

Hansen, James. "Game over for the Climate." *New York Times*, May 9, 2012. http://www.nytimes.com/2012/05/10/opinion/game-over-for-the-climate.html.

Jonsson, Patrik. "Gulf's $1.5 Trillion Oil Wildcat Play Marks Post-Spill Drilling 'Renaissance.'" *Christian Science Monitor*, September 14, 2013. http://www.csmonitor.com/USA/2013/0914/Gulf-s-1.5-trillion-oil-wildcat-play-marks-post-spill-drilling-renaissance.

Juhasz, Antonia. *The Tyranny of Oil: The World's Most Powerful Industry—and What We Must Do to Stop It*. New York: William Morrow, 2008.

Madrigal, Alexis. *Powering the Dream: The History and Promise of Green Technology*. Cambridge, MA: Da Capo Press, 2011.

McKibben, Bill. *Oil and Honey: The Education of an Unlikely Activity*. New York: Times Books, 2013.

Myre, Greg. "The 1973 Arab Oil Embargo: The Old Rules No Longer Apply." *NPR*, October 16, 2013. http://www.npr.org/blogs/parallels/2013/10/15/234771573/the-1973-arab-oil-embargo-the-old-rules-no-longer-apply.

Nguyen, Tuan C. "Scientists Turn Algae into Crude Oil in Less Than an Hour." *Smithsonian.com*, December 31, 2013. http://www.smithsonianmag.com/innovation/scientists-turn-algae-into-crude-oil-in-less-than-an-hour-180948282/?no-ist.

Rooney, Ben. "Big Oil's $38 Billion Defense." *CNN Money*, April 29, 2011. http://money.cnn.com/2011/04/29/news/companies/big-oil-gas-price-response/.

Safina, Carl. *A Sea in Flames: The Deepwater Horizon Oil Blowout*. New York: Crown, 2011.

Schulte, Bret. "Oil Spill Spotlights Keystone XL Issue: Is Canadian Crude Worse?" *National Geographic*, April 4, 2013. http://news.nationalgeographic.com/news/energy/2013/04/130405-arkansas-oil-spill-is-canadian-crude-worse/.

Smith, Matt. "Coast Guard, BP End Gulf Cleanup in 3 States." *CNN U.S.*, June 11, 2013. http://www.cnn.com/2013/06/10/us/gulf-oil-spill/.

Urbina, Ian. "U.S. Said to Allow Drilling without Needed Permits." *New York Times*, May 13, 2010. http://www.nytimes.com/2010/05/14/us/14agency.html?pagewanted=all.

Walsh, Bryan. "The Perils of Plastic." *Time*, April 1, 2010. http://content.time.com/time/specials/packages/article/0,28804,1976909_1976908_1976938,00.html.

Wilber, Tom. *Under the Surface: Fracking, Fortunes, and the Fate of the Marcellus Shale*. Ithaca, NY: Cornell University Press, 2012.

Yergin, Daniel. *The Prize: The Epic Quest for Oil, Money and Power*. New York: Simon & Schuster, 1992.

———. *The Quest: Energy, Security, and the Remaking of the Modern World*. New York: Penguin Press, 2011.

———. "There Will Be Oil." *Wall Street Journal*, September 17, 2011. http://online.wsj.com/news/articles/SB10001424053111904060604576572552998674340.

FOR FURTHER INFORMATION

BOOKS

Casper, Julie Kerr. *Fossil Fuels and Pollution: The Future of Air Quality*. New York: Facts on File, 2010.

Doeden, Matt. *Green Energy: Crucial Gains or Economic Strains?* Minneapolis: Twenty-First Century Books, 2010.

Haerens, Margaret. *Energy Alternatives*. Detroit: Greenhaven Press, 2013.

Marrin, Albert. *Black Gold: The Story of Oil in Our Lives*. New York: Knopf for Young Readers, 2013.

McPherson, Stephanie Sammartino. *Arctic Thaw: Climate Change and the Global Race for Energy Resources*. Minneapolis: Twenty-First Century Books, 2015.

Newman, Patricia. *Plastic, Ahoy! Investigating the Great Pacific Garbage Patch*. Minneapolis: Millbrook Press, 2014.

Tabak, John. *Coal and Oil*. New York: Facts on File, 2009.

Thompson, Tamara. *Fracking*. Detroit: Greenhaven Press, 2013.

WEBSITES

American Petroleum Institute
http://www.api.org
The national trade association for the US oil and gas industry offers a vast amount of information about oil and gas exploration, refining, transport, economics, and uses.

Arctic Sea Ice Decline
http://www.wunderground.com/climate/SeaIce.asp
This site from the forecasting organization Weather Underground gives facts and figures about the melting of sea ice in the Arctic region. The site includes statistics and climate change discussions.

Electric Vehicle Guide
http://content.sierraclub.org/evguide/
This site from the Sierra Club provides basic facts about electric vehicles, with information about batteries, fuel efficiency, carbon dioxide emissions, price, and more.

Global Climate Change
http://climate.nasa.gov
On this website, created by the National Aeronautics and Space Administration, visitors will learn about evidence that climate change has begun on Earth. The site discusses causes and effects of climate change, with statistics, images, and videos. It also includes discussions of renewable energy and an interactive page for kids.

Oil Change International
http://www.priceofoil.org
This national organization aims to expose the dangers of fossil fuels and to encourage the switch to clean energy.

Renewable Energy
http://energy.gov/science-innovation/energy-sources/renewable-energy
This site, created by the US Department of Energy, examines all sorts of renewable energy sources, including solar power, wind power, geothermal power, and hydropower.

Statistical Review of World Energy
http://www.bp.com/en/global/corporate/about-bp/energy-economics/statistical-review-of-world-energy.html
Created by the oil company BP, this website provides extensive data about global energy use, with breakdowns by country, region, energy type, and other categories.

350.org
http://350.org
Cofounded by author and environmentalist Bill McKibben, 350.org wants to keep Earth livable for humans, plants, and animals by reducing the amount of carbon dioxide in the atmosphere below 350 parts per million. The organization has spearheaded a number of activist campaigns, including the fight to stop expansion of the Keystone XL pipeline.

Unfracktured: Joining Together to Fight Fracking
http://earthjustice.org/advocacy-campaigns/unfracktured
The environmental organization Earth Justice created this website, which shines a spotlight on hydraulic fracturing and its threats to land, water, and health.

US Energy Information Administration
http://www.eia.gov
This US government agency offers extensive statistics and other data on various types of energy, including oil and gas as well as alternative fuels.

MOVIES

Bidder 70. DVD. Telluride, CO: Gage & Gage Productions, 2012.
This award-winning film tells the story of Tim DeChristopher, who took a stand to prevent the sale of federal lands to oil and gas companies, served two years in prison for his actions, and became a spokesperson in the fight against climate change.

Crude: The Real Price of Oil. DVD. New York: First Run Features, 2009.
In Ecuador, thirty thousand indigenous rain forest dwellers took on the US oil giant Texaco (which later merged with Chevron), charging that the company had contaminated their homeland in the Amazon jungle with decades of oil extraction. This documentary film traces the legal fight between the Ecuadorean Davids and the Big Oil Goliath.

Gasland. DVD. New York: HBO Documentary Films, 2011.
This documentary film shines a light on the natural gas boom in the United States. It examines the negative effects of hydraulic fracturing, which contaminates water and air. A sequel, *Gasland II*, explains how powerful energy companies use their financial clout to influence politicians and government policy.

Greasy Rider. DVD. New York: Sundial Pictures, 2006.
In this documentary, the filmmakers drive their 1981 Mercedes-Benz cross-country, stopping at restaurants along the way to fill up on free fuel made from kitchen grease. The film also examines the larger questions of fossil fuel extraction and its harmful effects.

INDEX

ABOUT THE AUTHOR

Margaret J. Goldstein was born in Detroit and graduated from the University of Michigan. She has written and edited many books for young adult readers. She lives in northern New Mexico.

PHOTO ACKNOWLEDGMENTS